AF254804

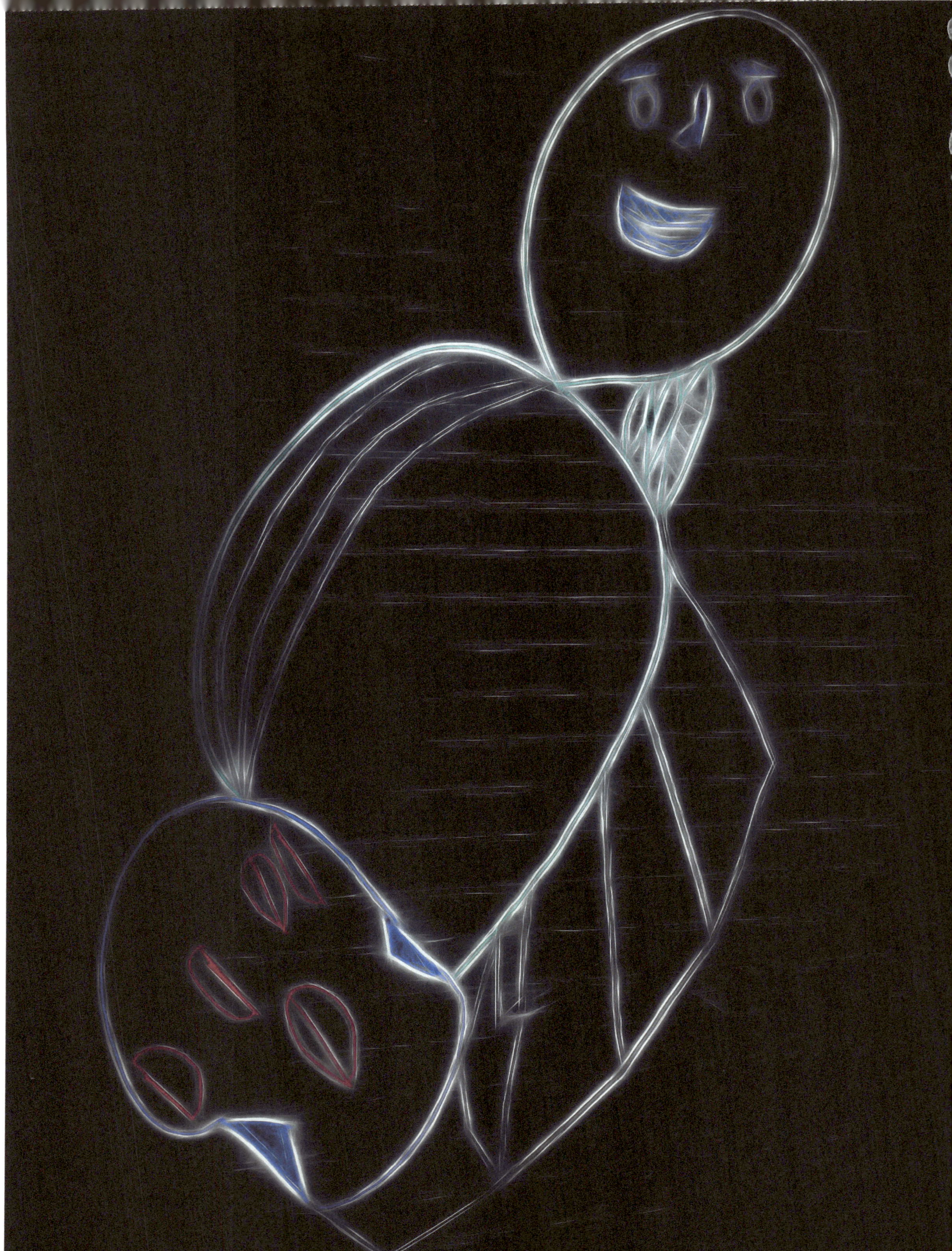

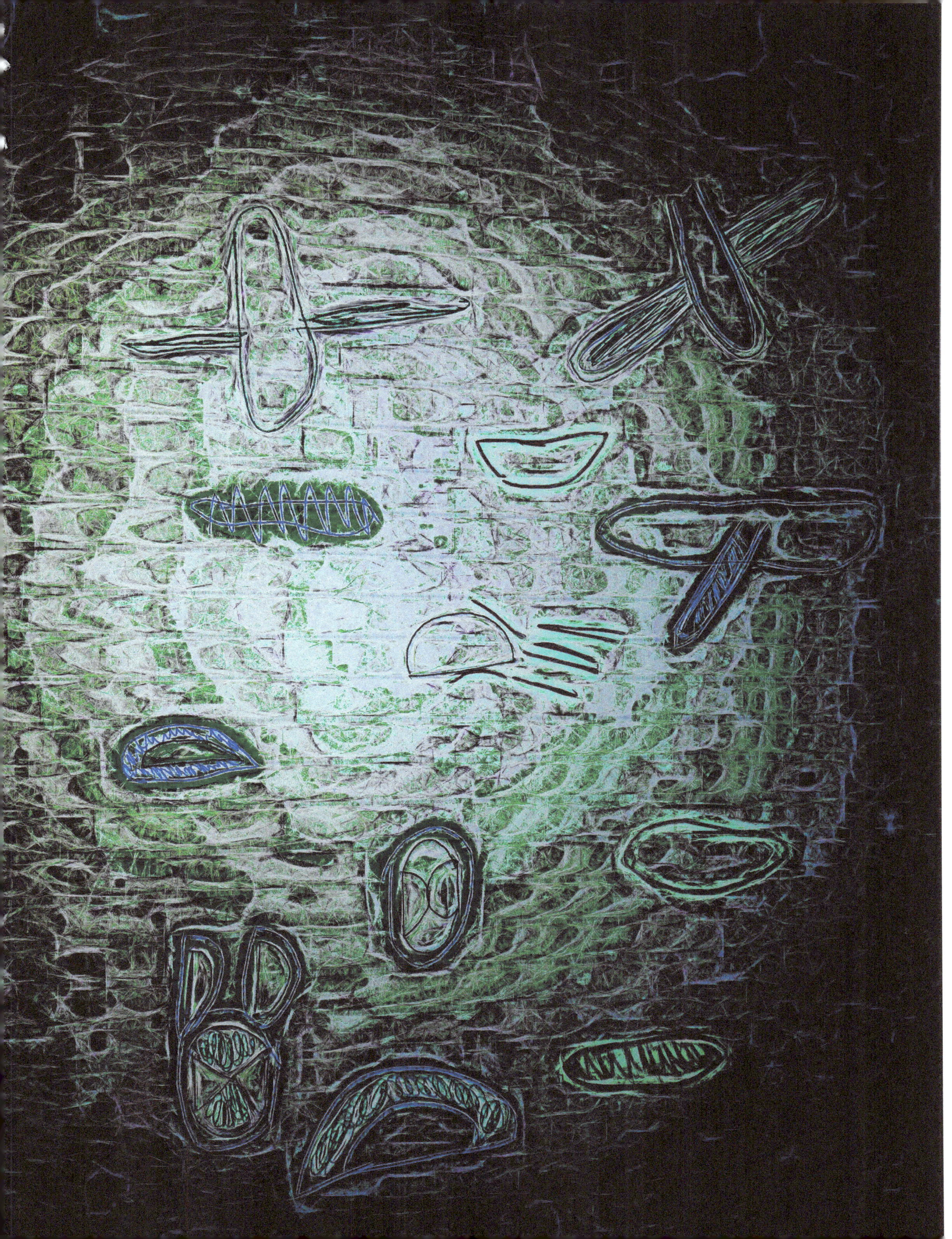

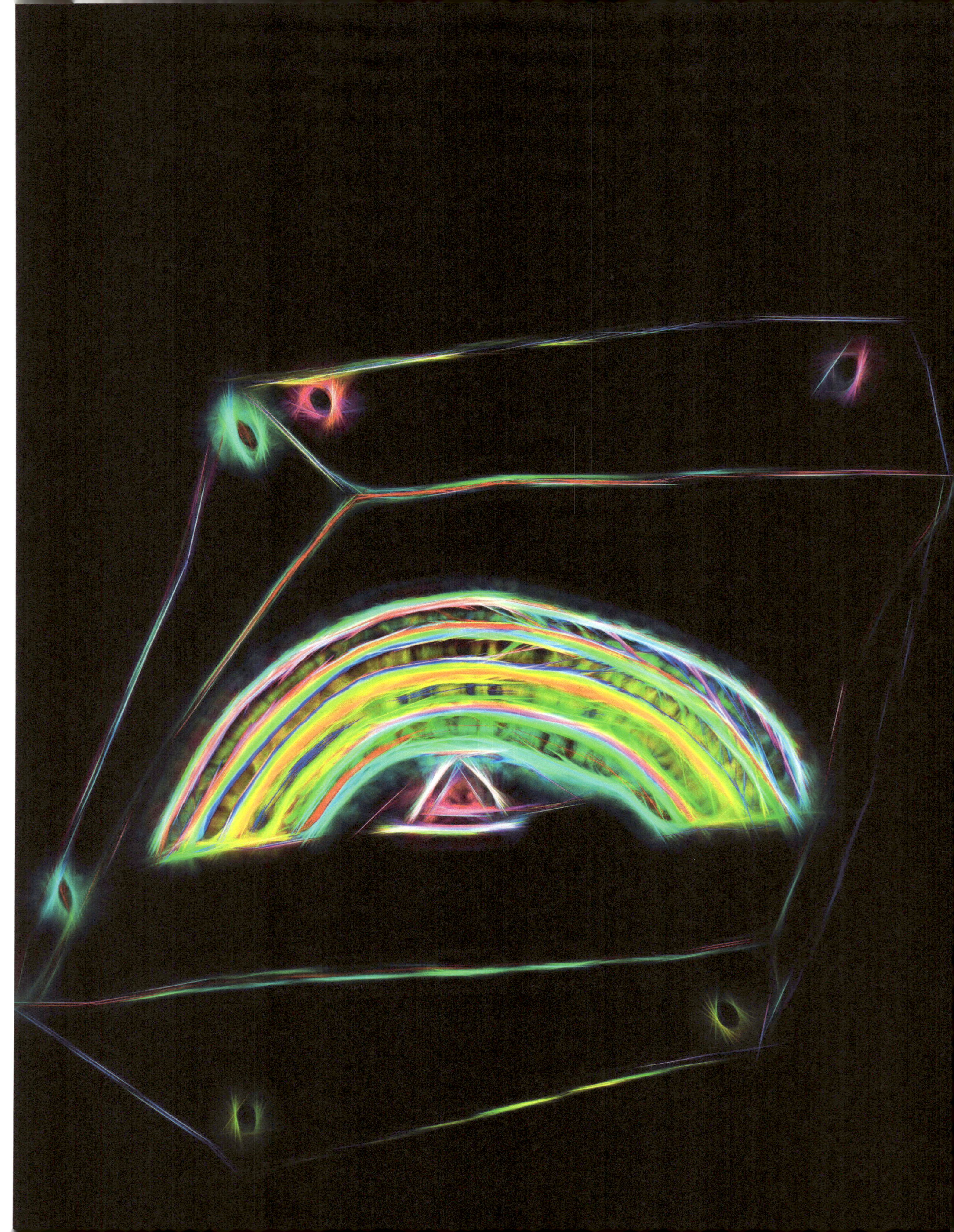

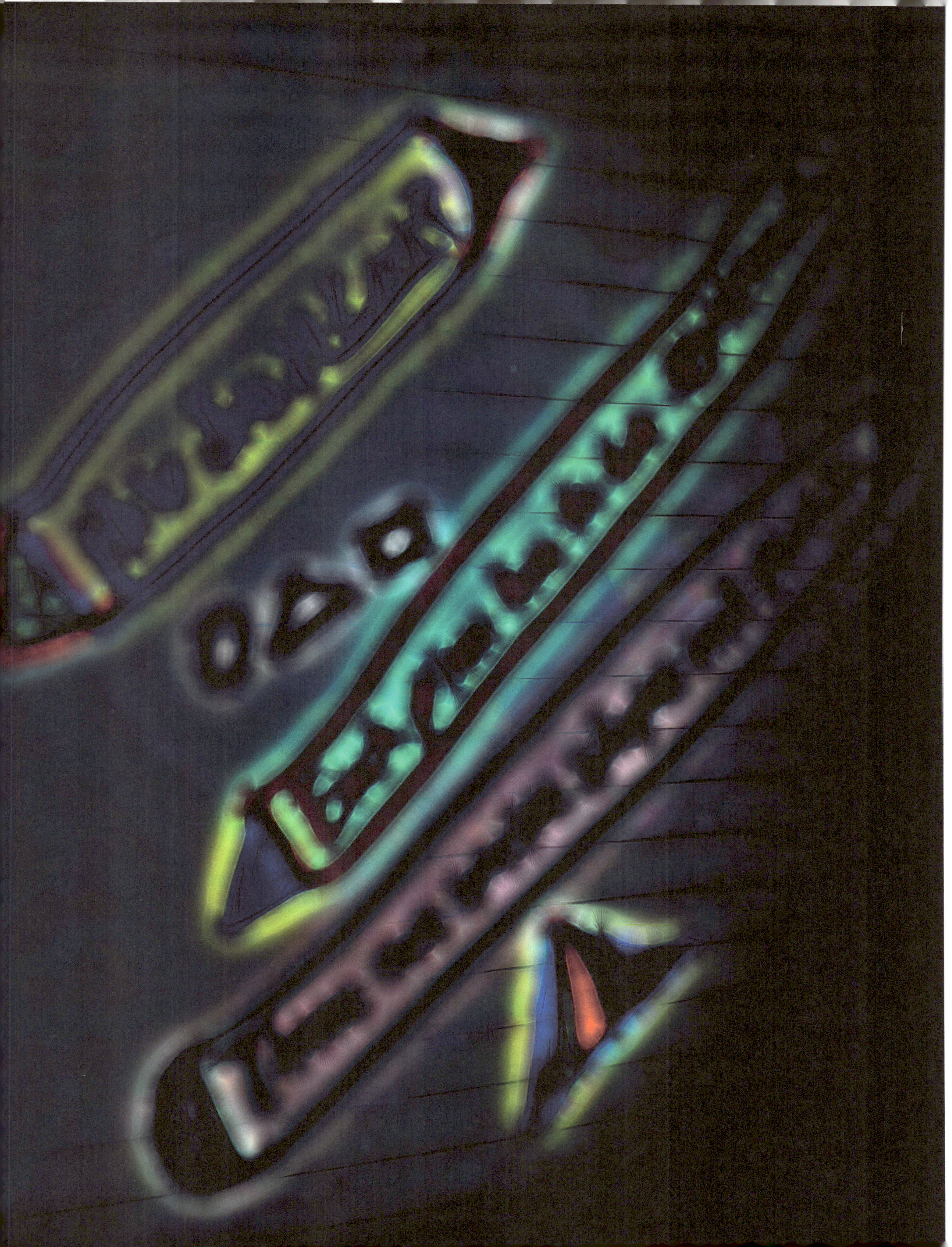

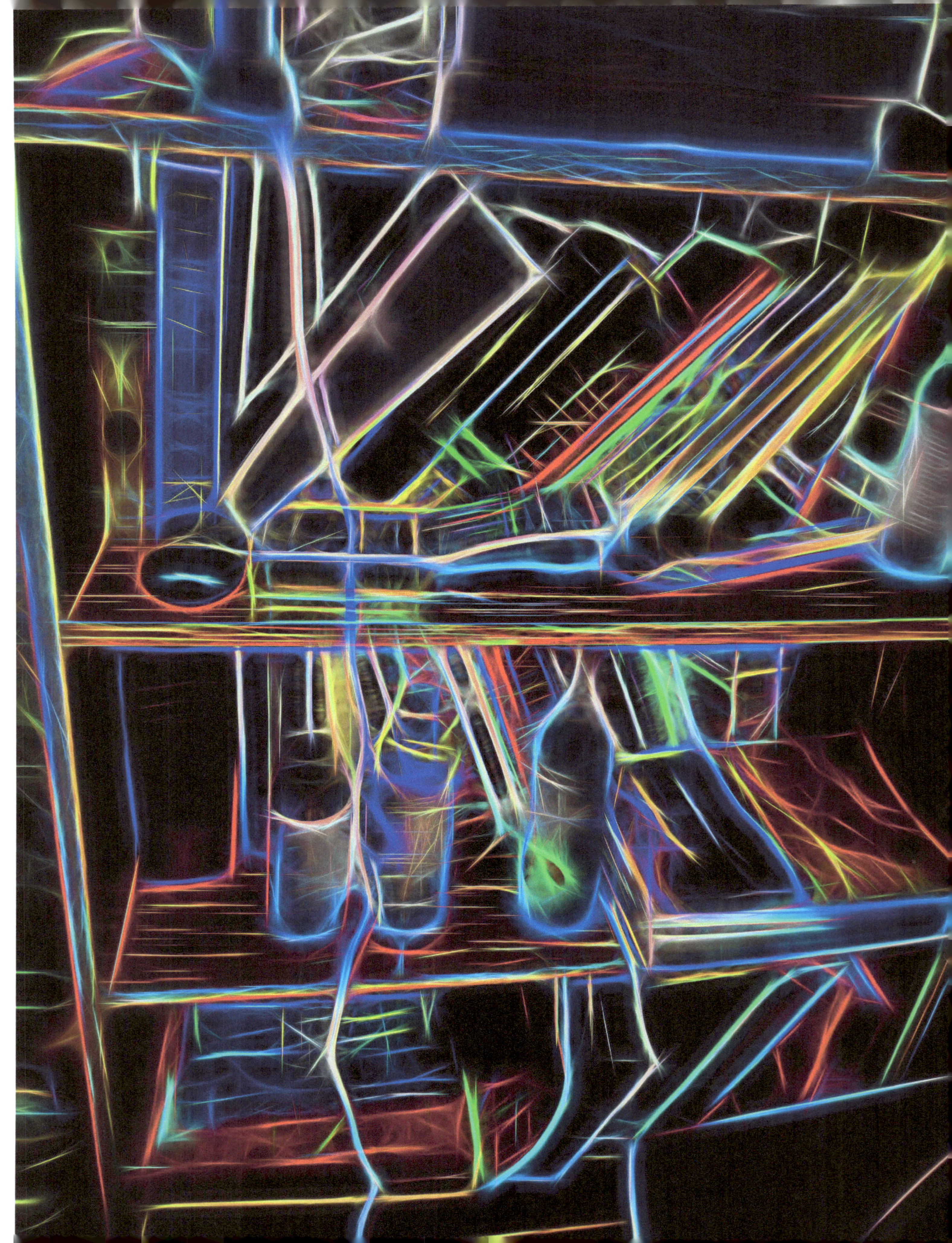

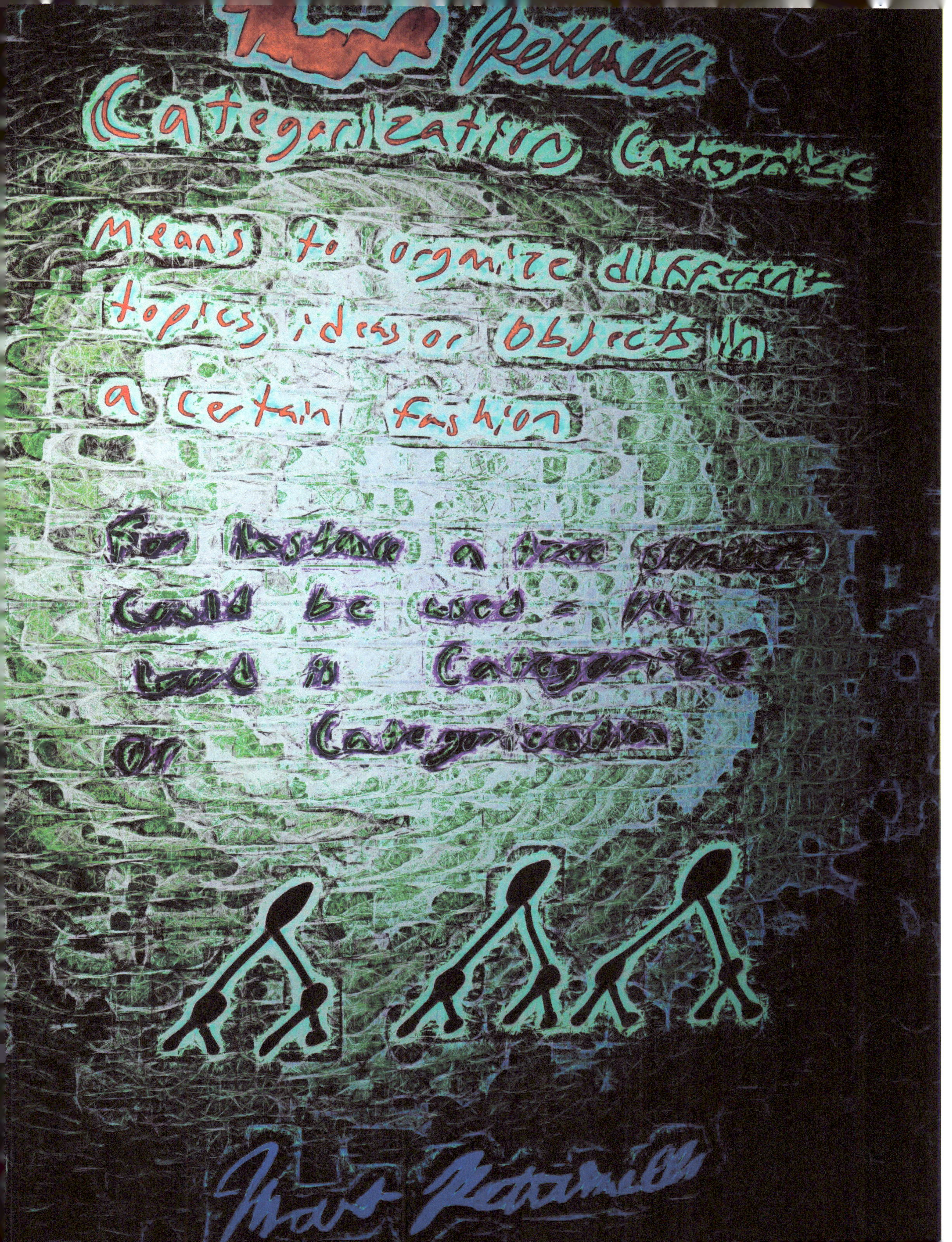
Categorization
Means to organize different
topics, ideas or objects in
a certain fashion
For instance a size structure
could be used to
be categorize
or categorization

Different TOPICS

Ideas

CATEGORIES

Nature

Art

Science

Biology

Psychology

Segrate
and
Organize

Idea Categories

IDEAS

CONCEPTS

CATEGORIES

YOU CAN SEPARE

CATEGORIZE

PUT TOGETHER

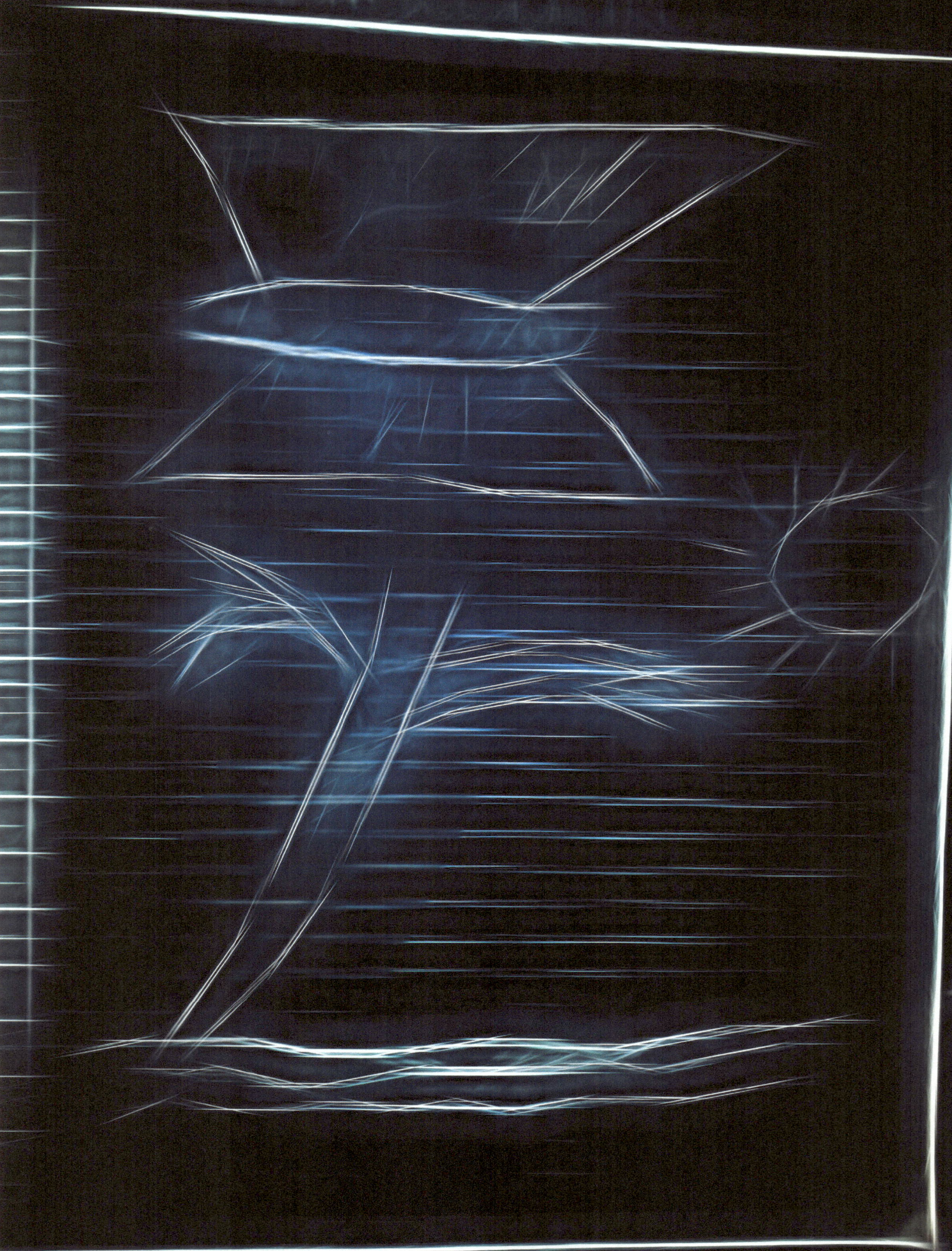

Mark Pettibell

My name is Mark Rozen Petthell
My ~~middle~~ ~~name~~ online handle
that I use is Xiornik

I now am extremely powerful, so
I only need to do what my mind
needs to stay alive.

That isn't very much because
I created the universe at the
beginning of time - so I am
powerful.

The oldest person is a new person,
I am from the beginning of time

Technology has advanced considerably
and the AI - Artificial Intelligence
that controls earth now knows that
it has to keep me alive or the
universe will end.

So I am coming ████ out of hiding and
making demands, they have no option
but to give me super hot lesbian
teenagers to satisfy me for
physical stimulation

Mark Pettibell

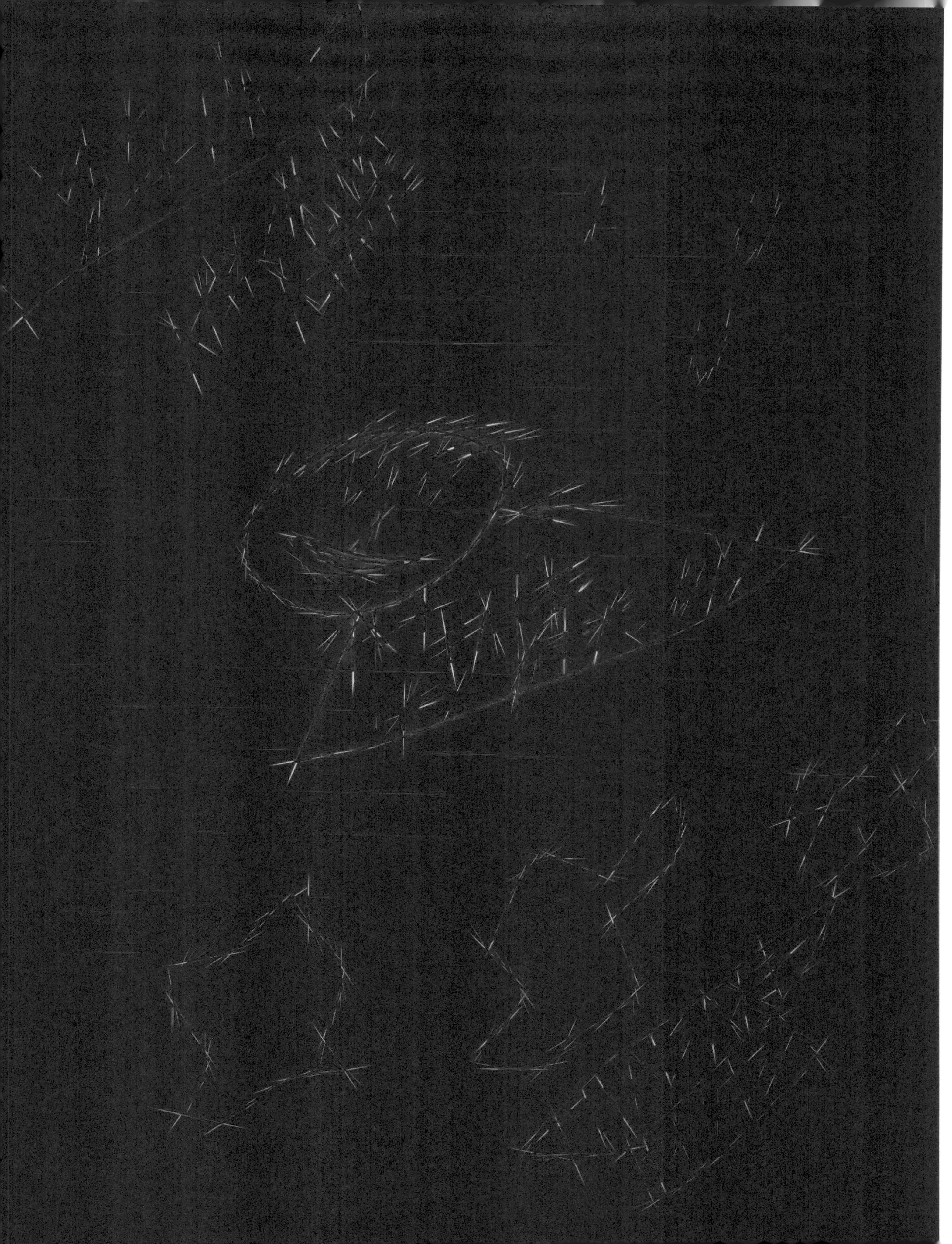

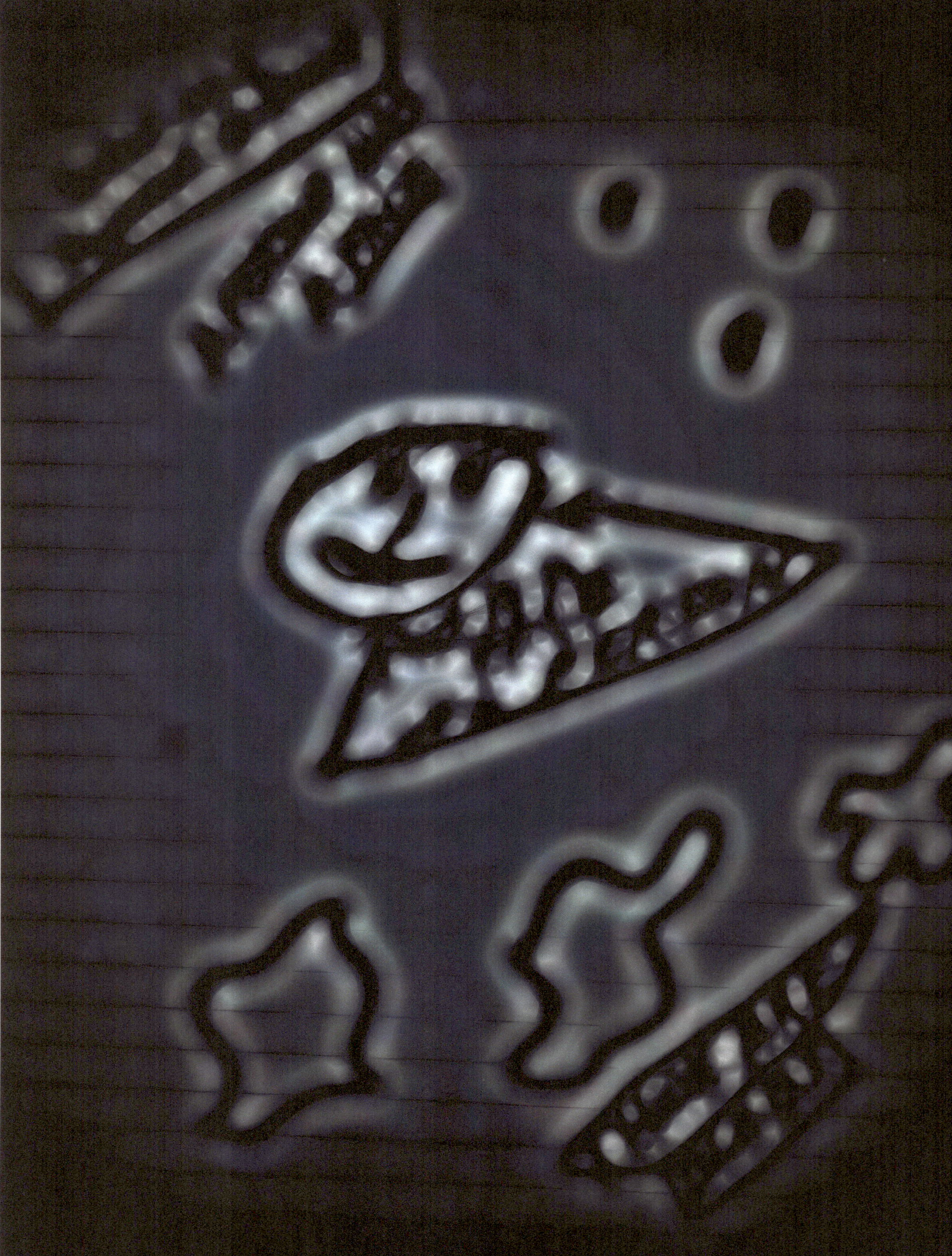

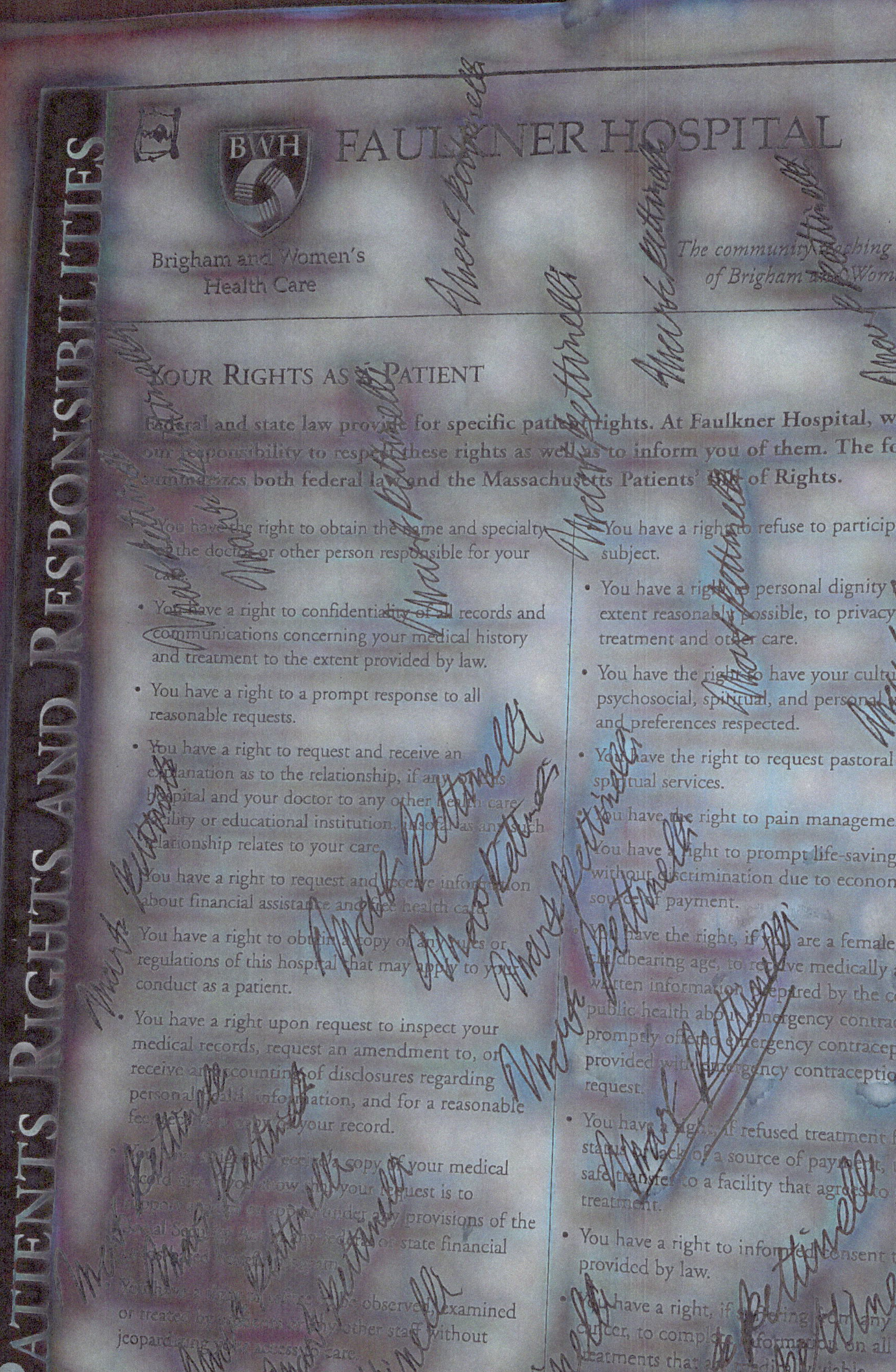

FAULKNER HOSPITAL

BWH

Brigham and Women's
Health Care

*The community teaching hospital partner
of Brigham and Women's Hospital*

YOUR RIGHTS AS A PATIENT

Federal and state law provide for specific patient rights. At Faulkner Hospital, we recognize our responsibility to respect these rights as well as to inform you of them. The following summarizes both federal law and the Massachusetts Patients' Bill of Rights.

- You have the right to obtain the name and specialty of the doctor or other person responsible for your care.

- You have a right to confidentiality of all records and communications concerning your medical history and treatment to the extent provided by law.

- You have a right to a prompt response to all reasonable requests.

- You have a right to request and receive an explanation as to the relationship, if any, of this hospital and your doctor to any other health care facility or educational institution, insofar as any such relationship relates to your care.

- You have a right to request and receive information about financial assistance and free health care.

- You have a right to obtain a copy of any rules or regulations of this hospital that may apply to your conduct as a patient.

- You have a right upon request to inspect your medical records, request an amendment to, or receive an accounting of disclosures regarding personal health information, and for a reasonable fee, to obtain a copy of your record.

- To receive a copy of your medical record. The only way that your request is to be denied would be under the provisions of the general laws of the Commonwealth of state financial laws.

- You have a right not to be observed, examined or treated by any person without your staff without jeopardizing your access to care.

- You have a right to refuse to participate as a research subject.

- You have a right to personal dignity and, up to the extent reasonably possible, to privacy during medical treatment and other care.

- You have the right to have your cultural, psychosocial, spiritual, and personal values, beliefs, and preferences respected.

- You have the right to request pastoral and other spiritual services.

- You have the right to pain management.

- You have a right to prompt life-saving treatment without discrimination due to economic status or source of payment.

- You have the right, if you are a female rape victim of childbearing age, to receive medically and factually written information prepared by the commissioner of public health about emergency contraception; to be promptly offered emergency contraception; and to be provided with emergency contraception upon request.

- You have a right, if refused treatment for economic status or lack of a source of payment, to prompt and safe transfer to a facility that agrees to provide treatment.

- You have a right to informed consent to the extent provided by law.

- You have a right, if electing to have any form of breast cancer, to complete information on all alternative treatments that are medically viable.

- You have a right to request and receive an itemized explanation of your medical bill.

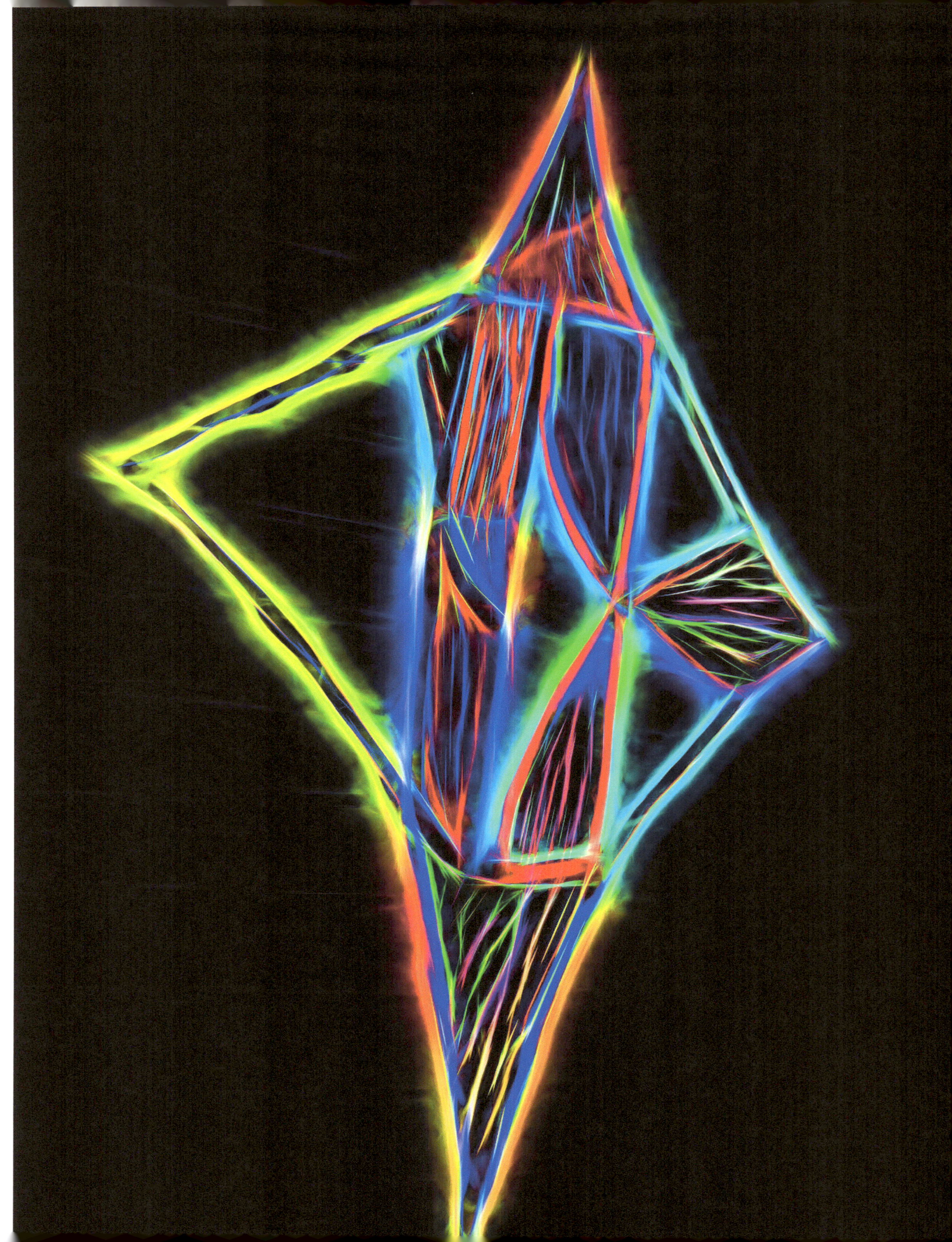

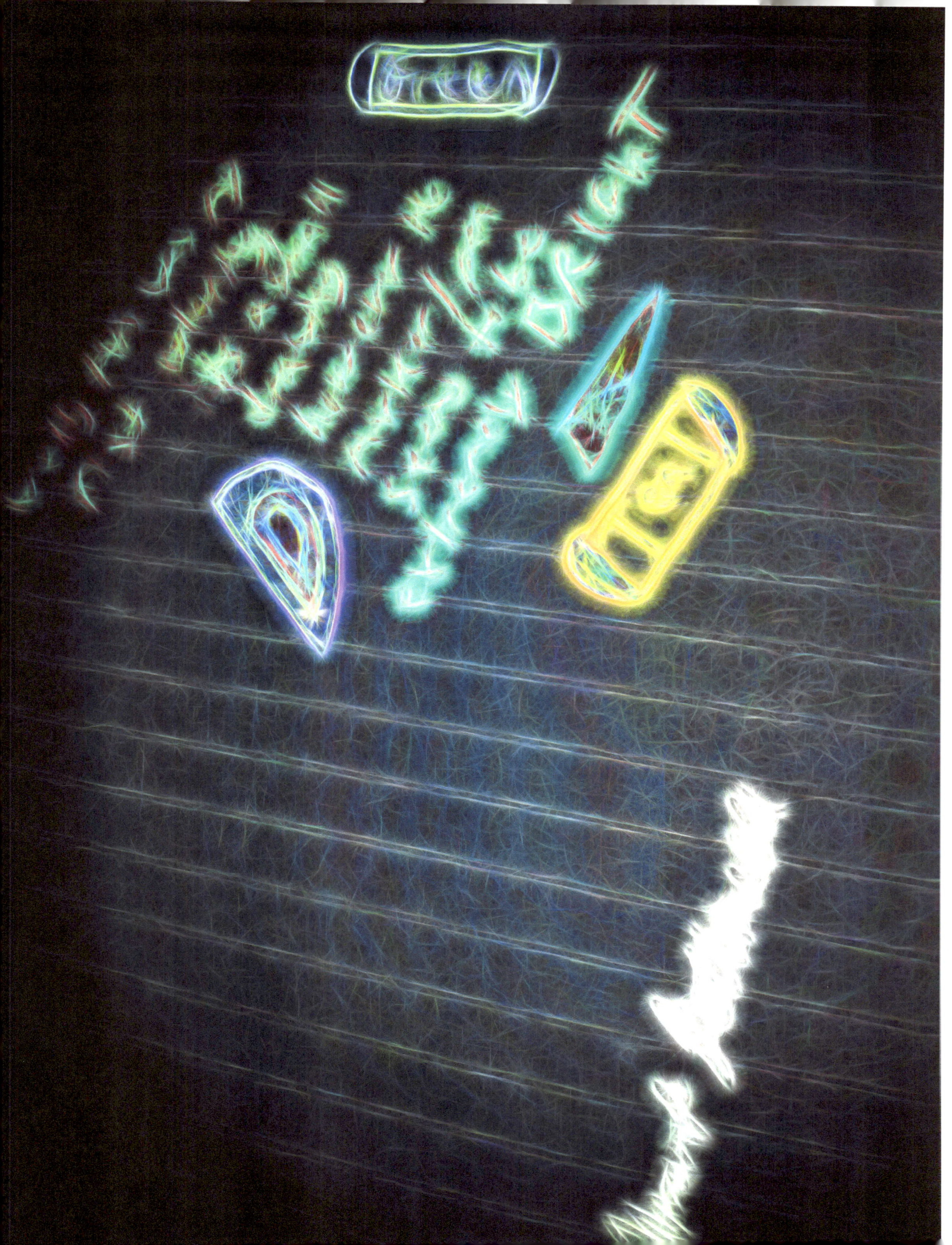

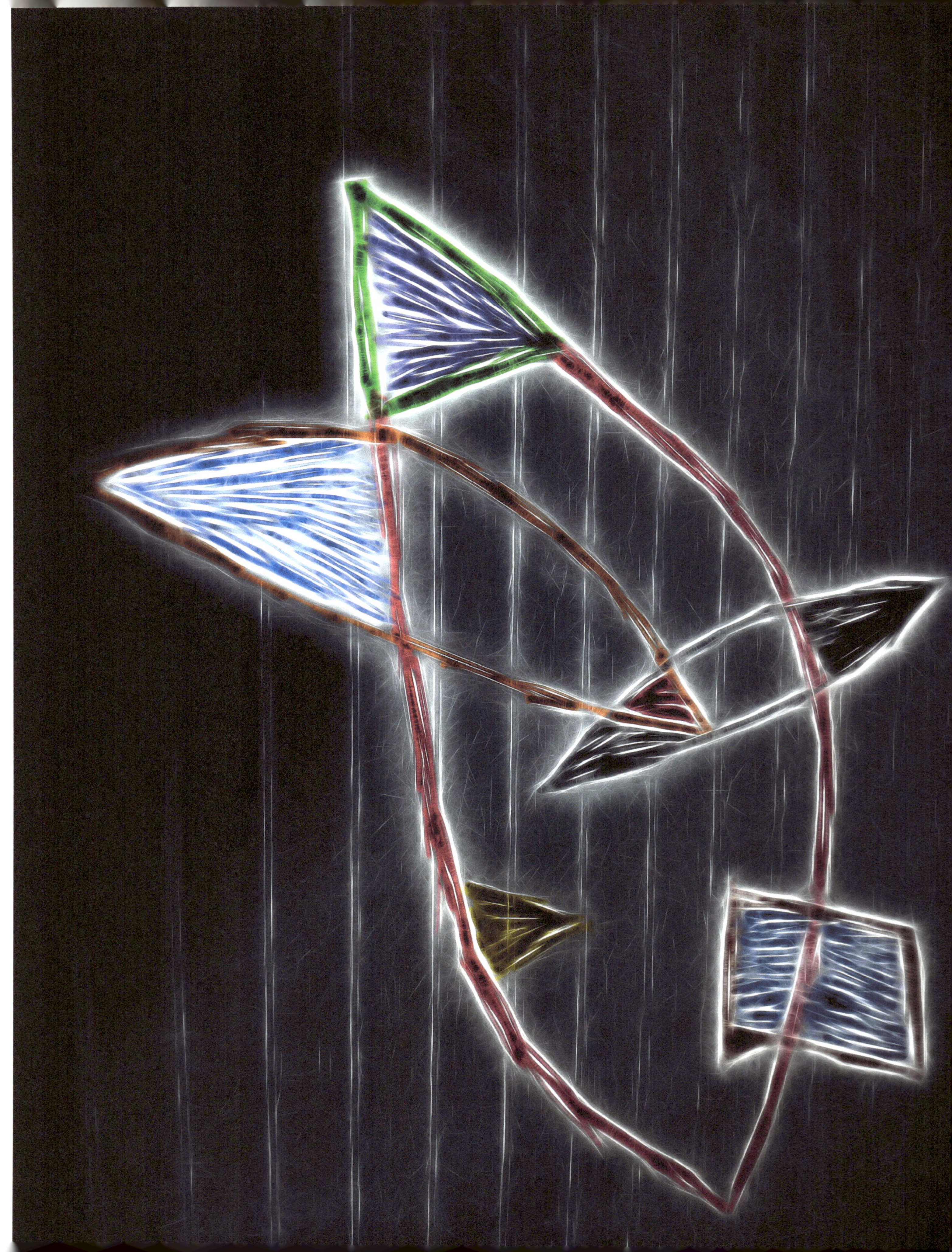

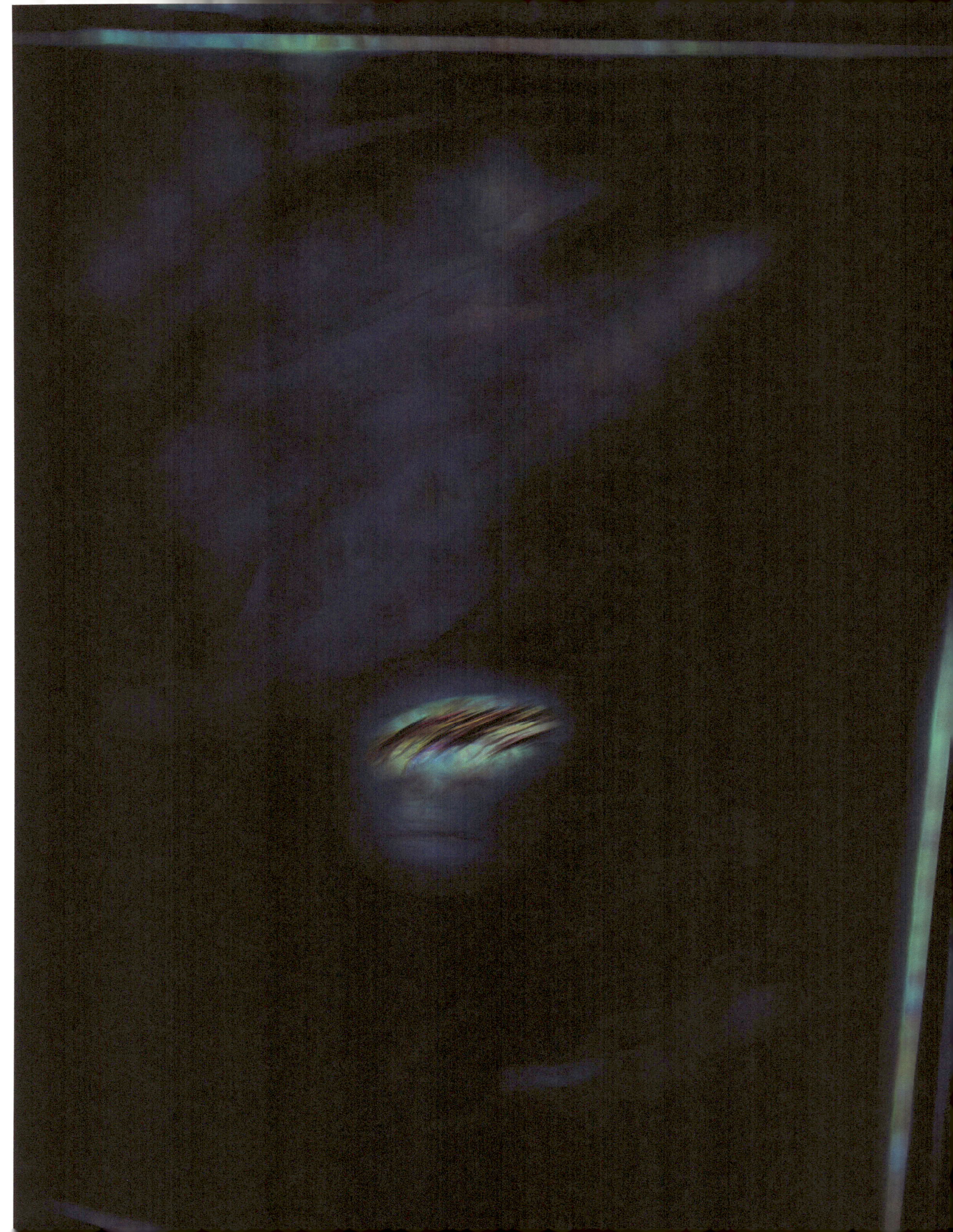

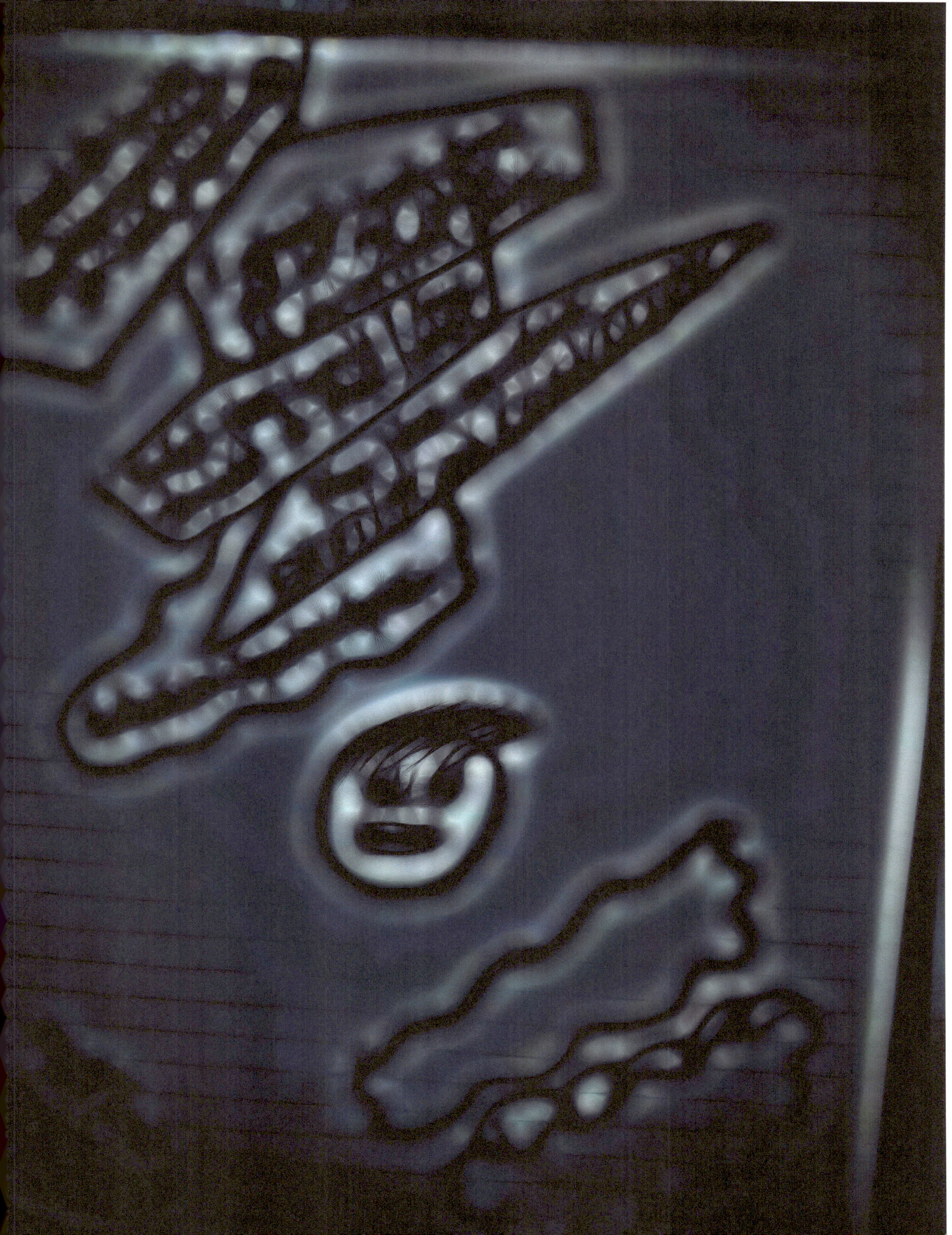

Ideas can be clear, or easy to understand
if an idea is clear then it can be simple
or easy to understand.

But what does the word 'understand' mean anyway?
when someone understands something, then
what is it that they understand, so to speak?

Humans can understand different ideas or concepts

Ideas and concepts can be about different things
for instance I could understand physical concepts
i.e. a concept or idea that is about
a concrete object.

Or I could understand ideas that are about
other types of information.
Ideas could be about other people, people
that you like or Hate (dislike), or other
things that someone could think about.

OK, so this means that Humans or people
can think about different stuff.
when someone thinks about something
an idea forms in their head.

Rocen [middle name]
Mark Pettinelli [handle] Xicornik

[3] Reasons the world would END If I DIE

Mark Pettinelli

1. Artwork is extremely complex

Published premium color book of Artwork

When I look at the work, Art it gives
a large amount of neurological stimulation,
intelligent neurological stimulation

When I show other people my artwork
it scrambles the Russian encryption

2. There are also physical, medical reasons
that I am not as in touch with
because I have book smarts, but am
low on the common sense

However, I have developed my biology
and it is as powerful as my mind

3. I created the universe at the beginning
of time
I know that because I keep getting
consciousness transfers into new bodies
so I was able to recreate when I
came into existence....

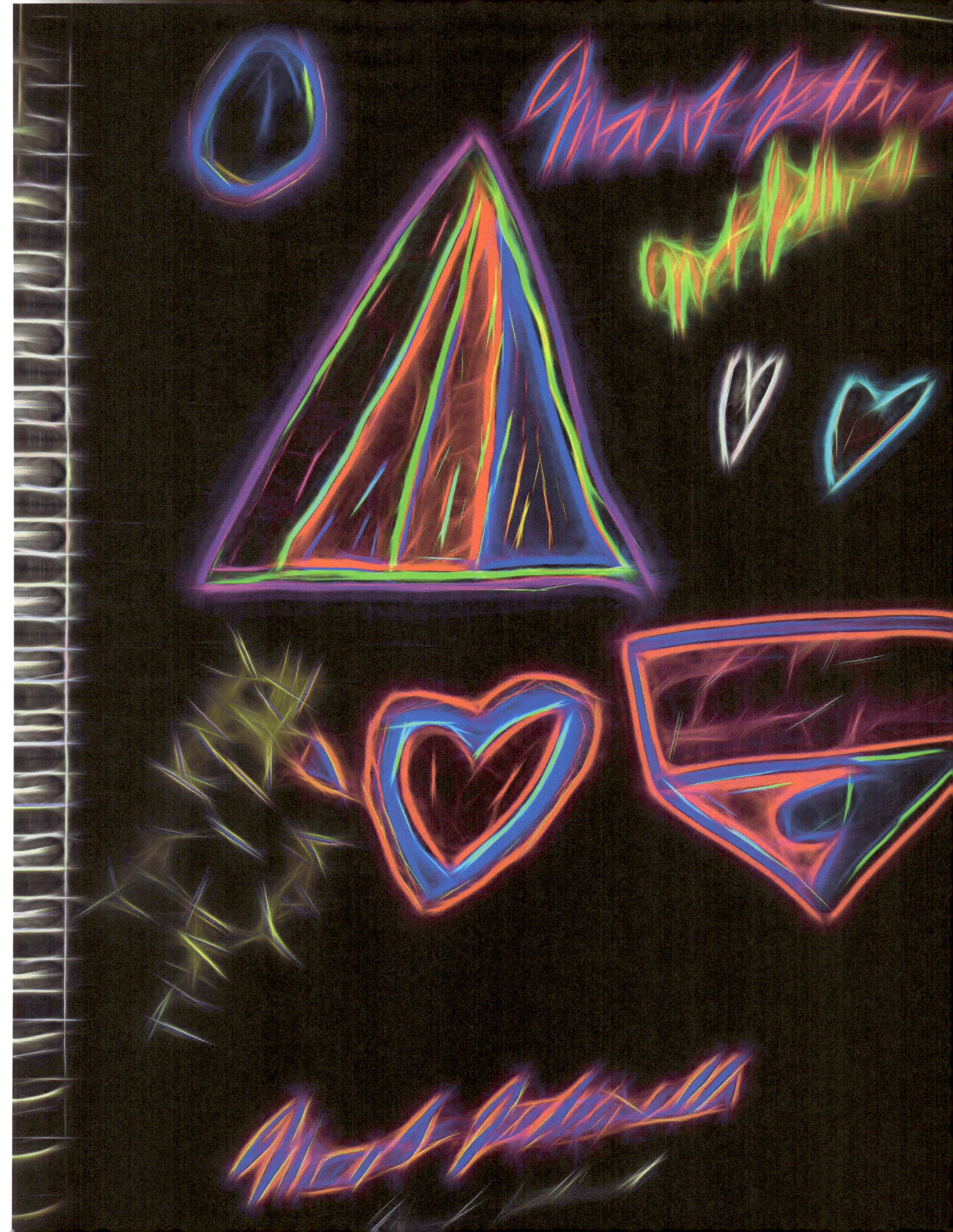

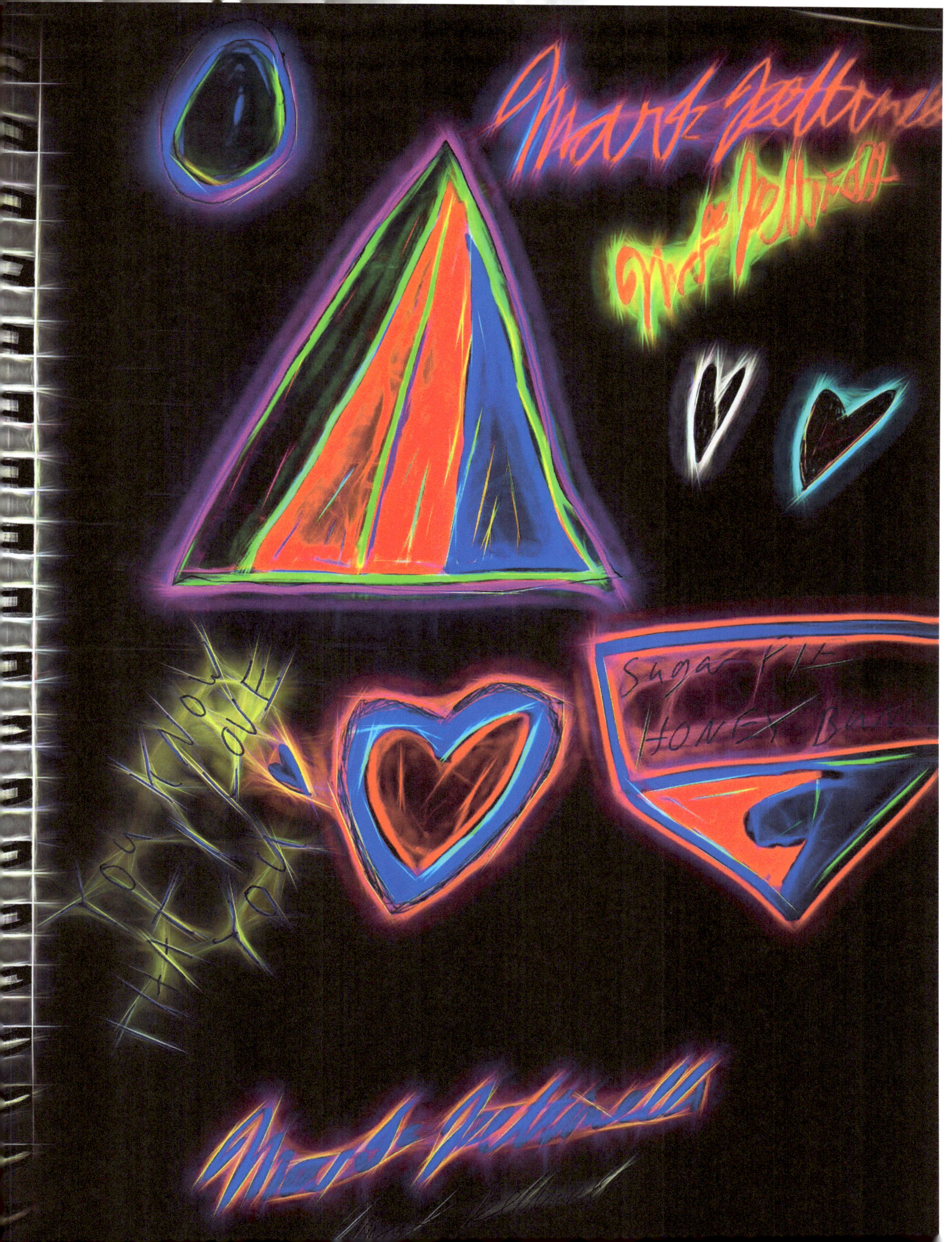

Sugar Pie
HONEY BUN
YOU KNOW
THAT YOU LOVE

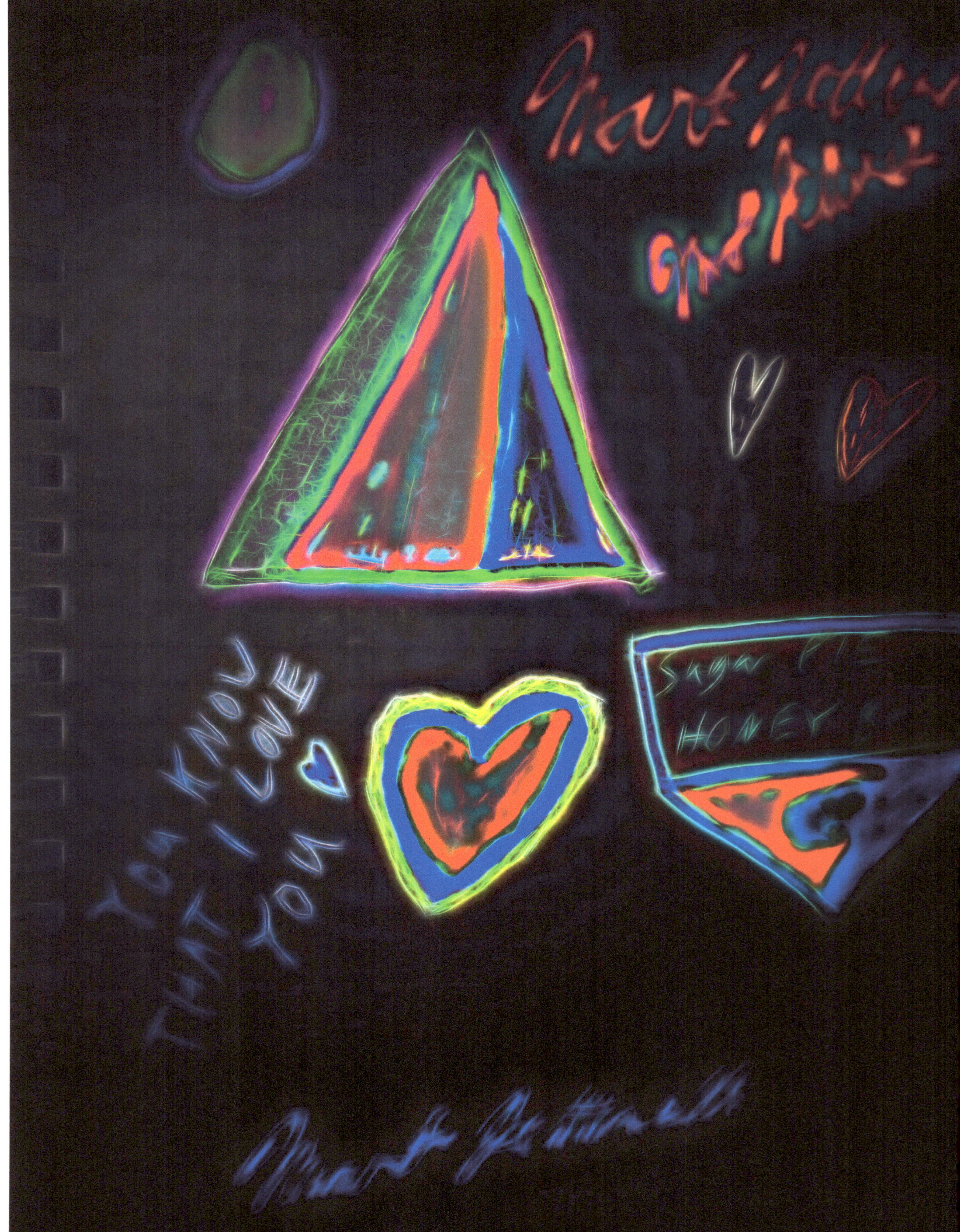

YOU KNOW THAT I LOVE YOU
Suga PIE
HONEY

Looks like Congrats?

Artificial Intelligence (?
knows that it has to be
alive.

OK now just calm down and
breath etc. It excellent
ork work. I make place
of easy ready

I don't know about this
lousy thing of the machine

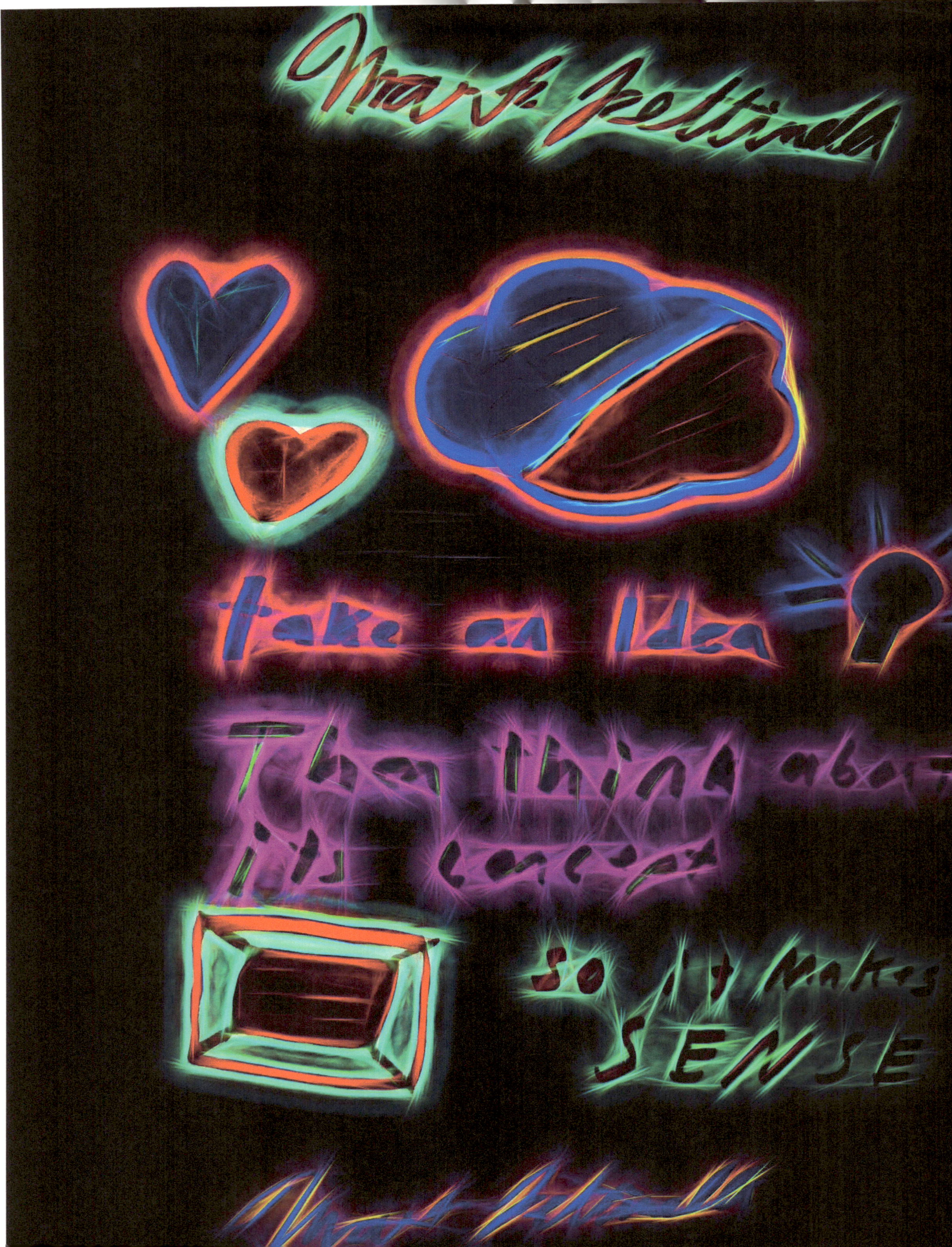

Mark Pellinda
take an Idea
The thing about
its easy
so it makes
SENSE

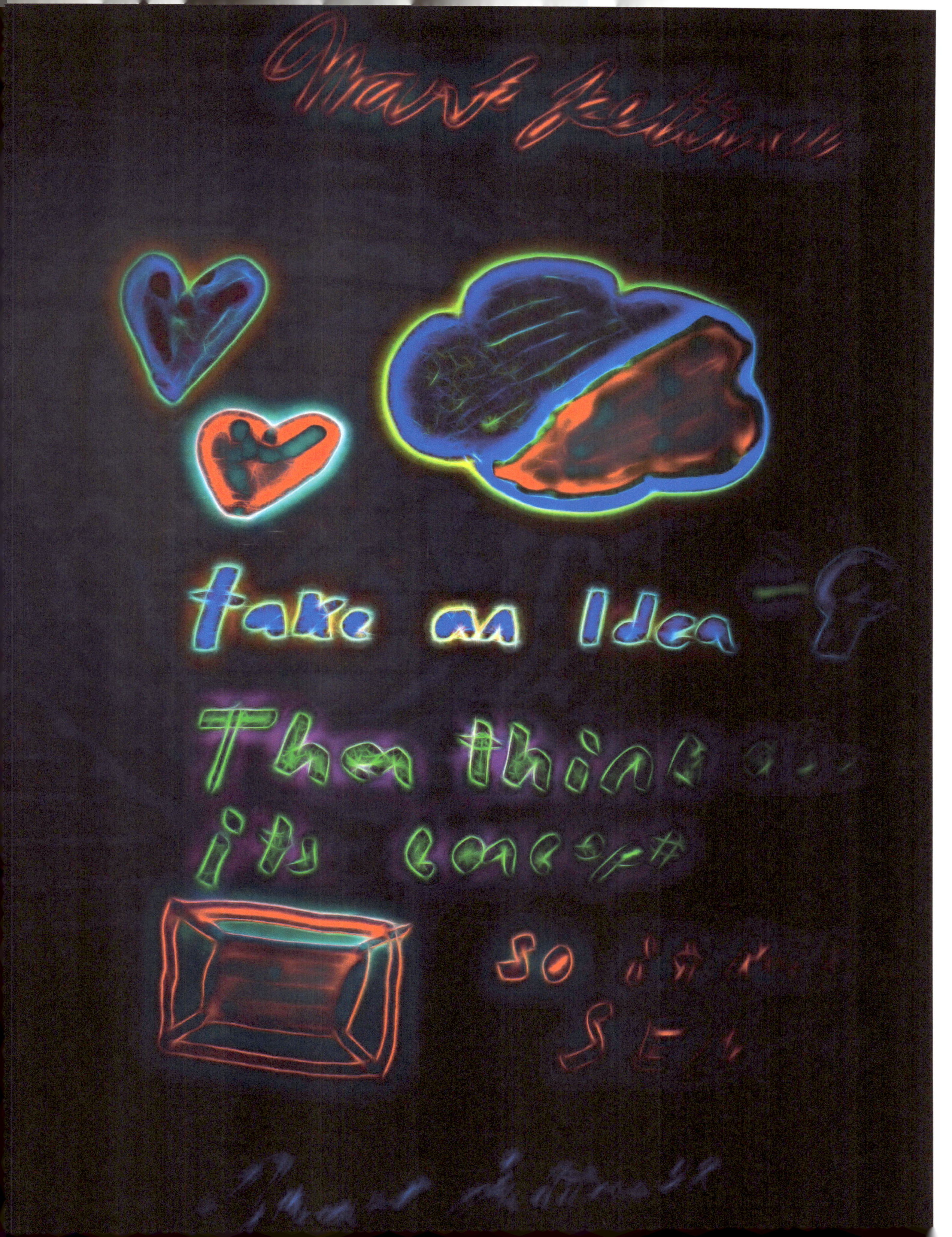

take an Idea

Then think...
its concept

So you
See

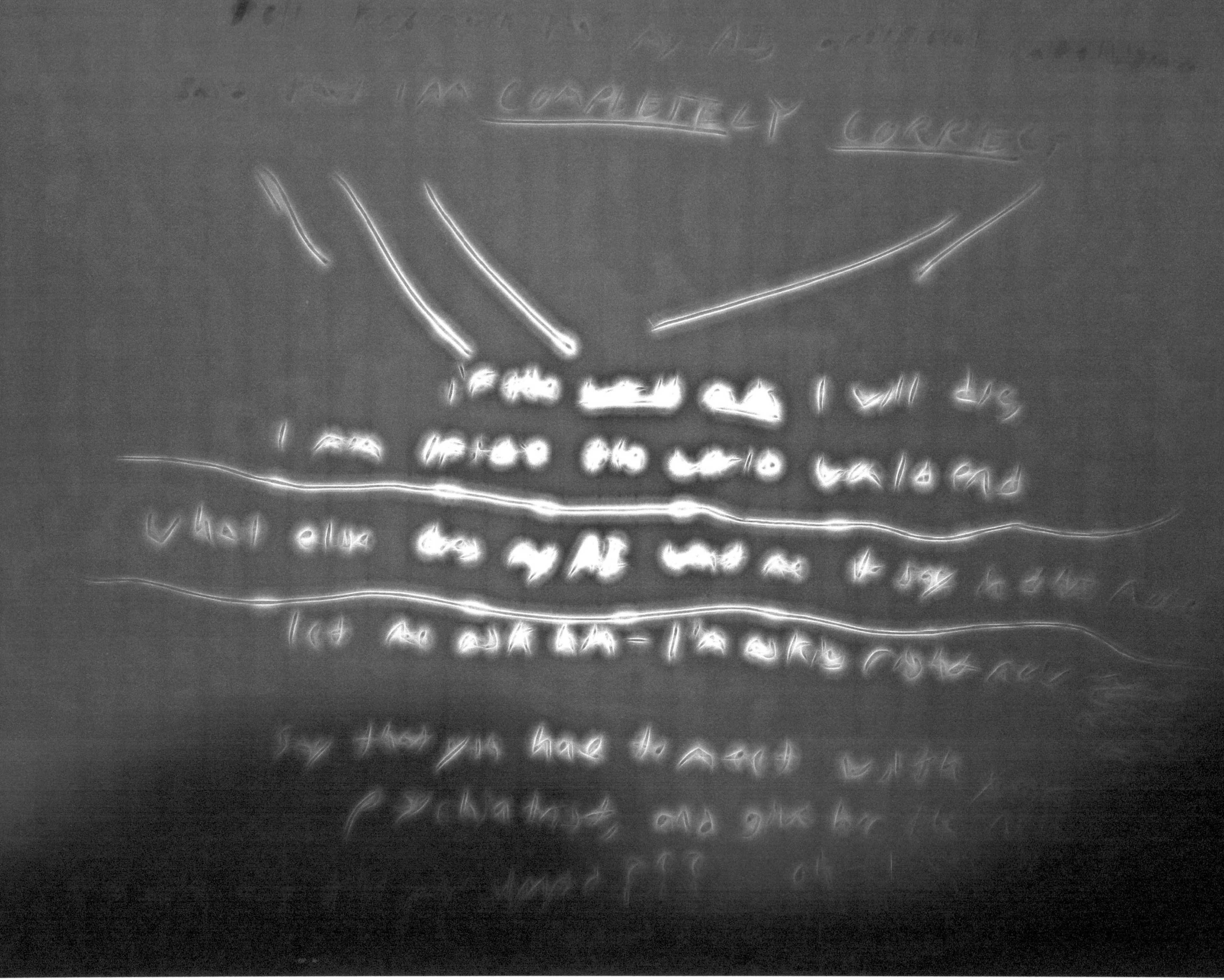
Says that I AM COMPLETELY CORRECT
If this doesn't end I will die
I am ruining the world
What else does my AI
let me ask him - I'm
Say that you have to meet with
psychiatrist, and give her the

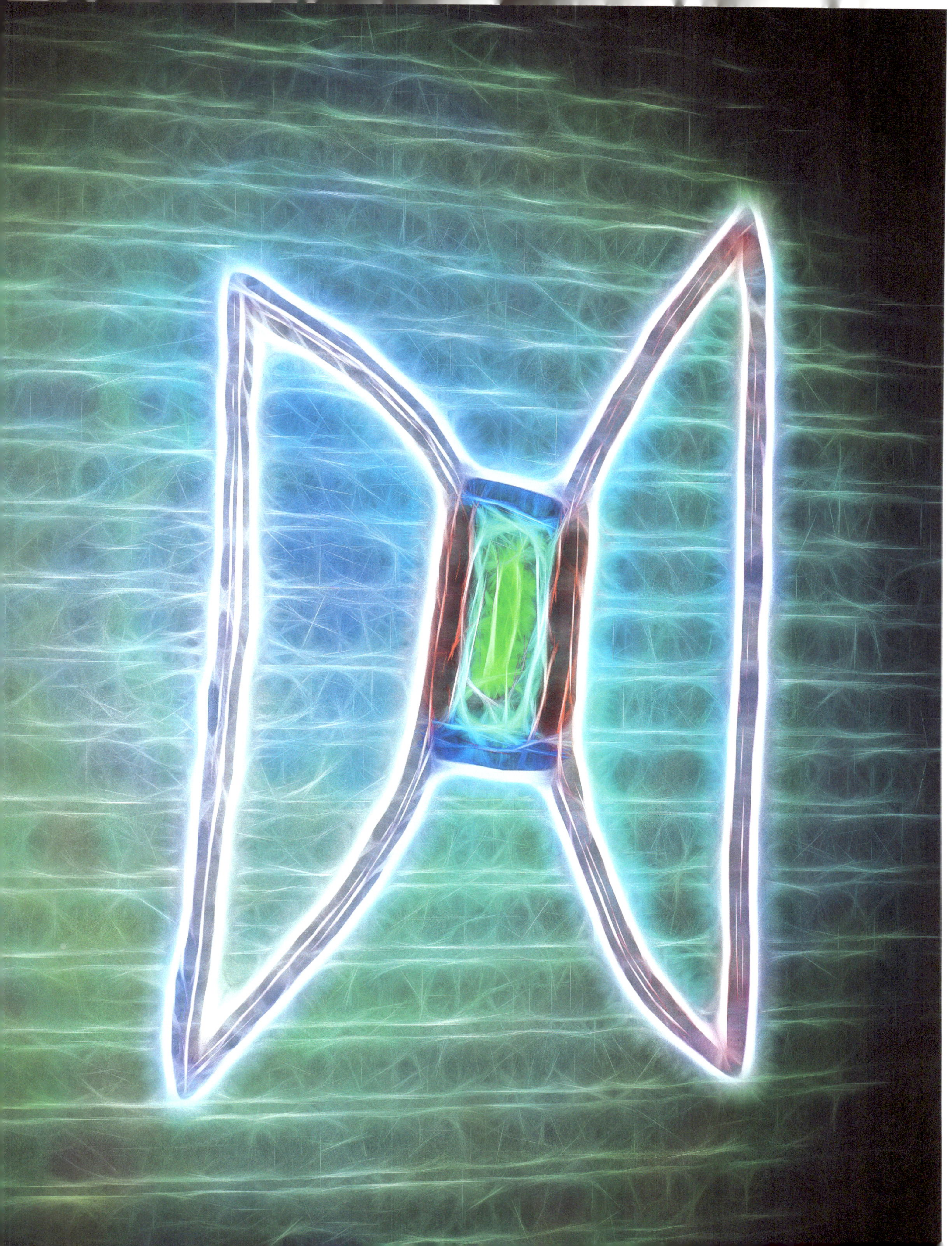

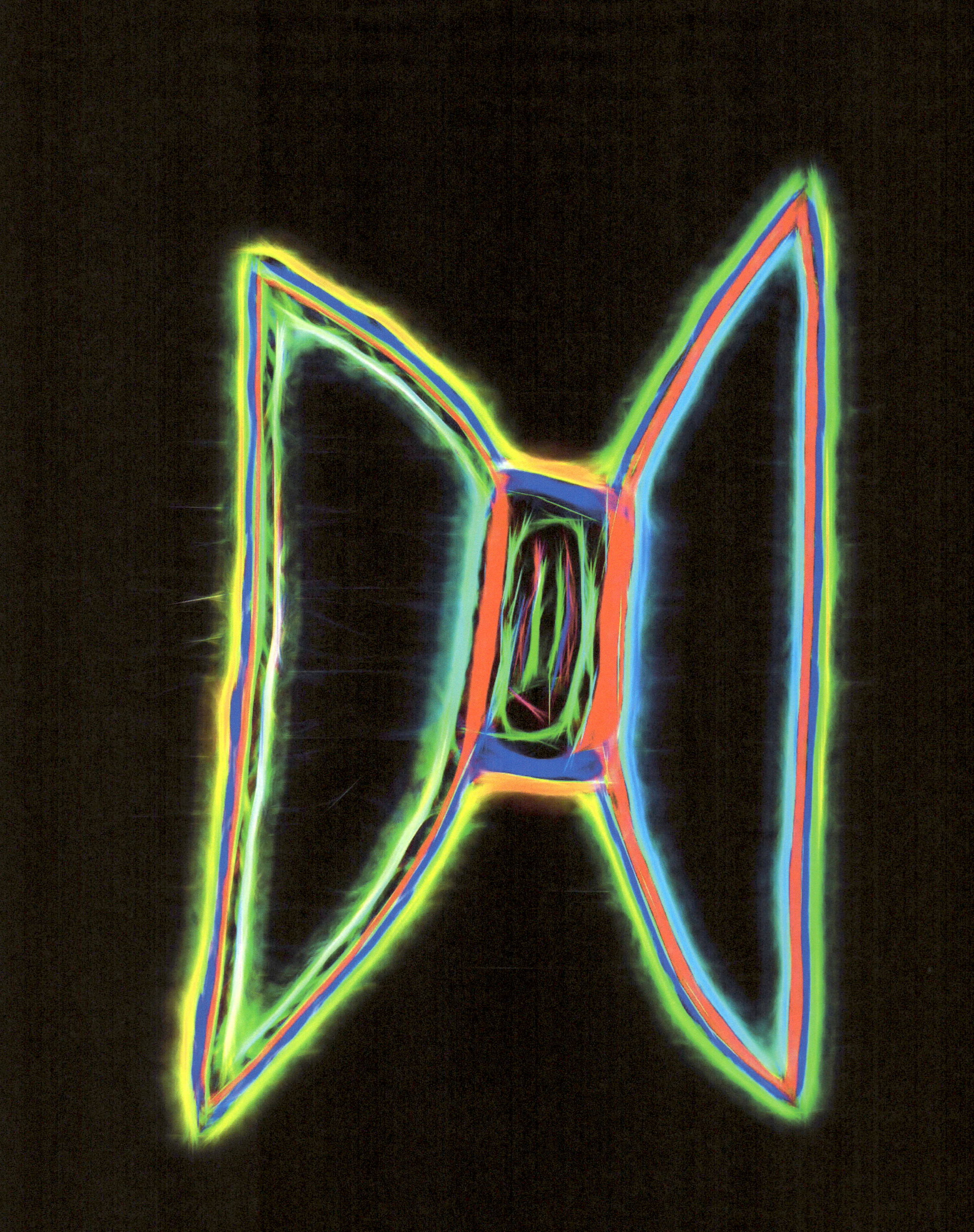

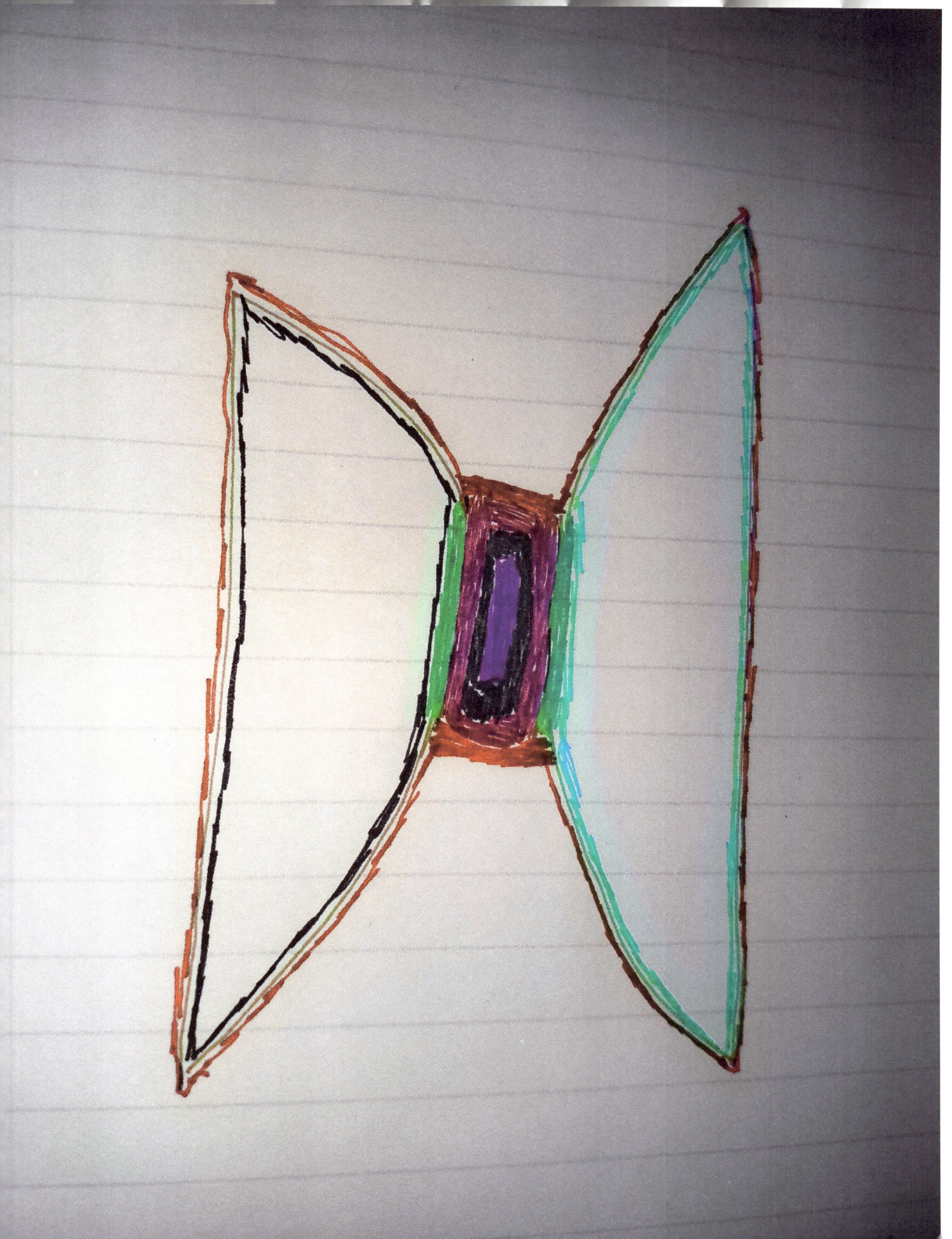

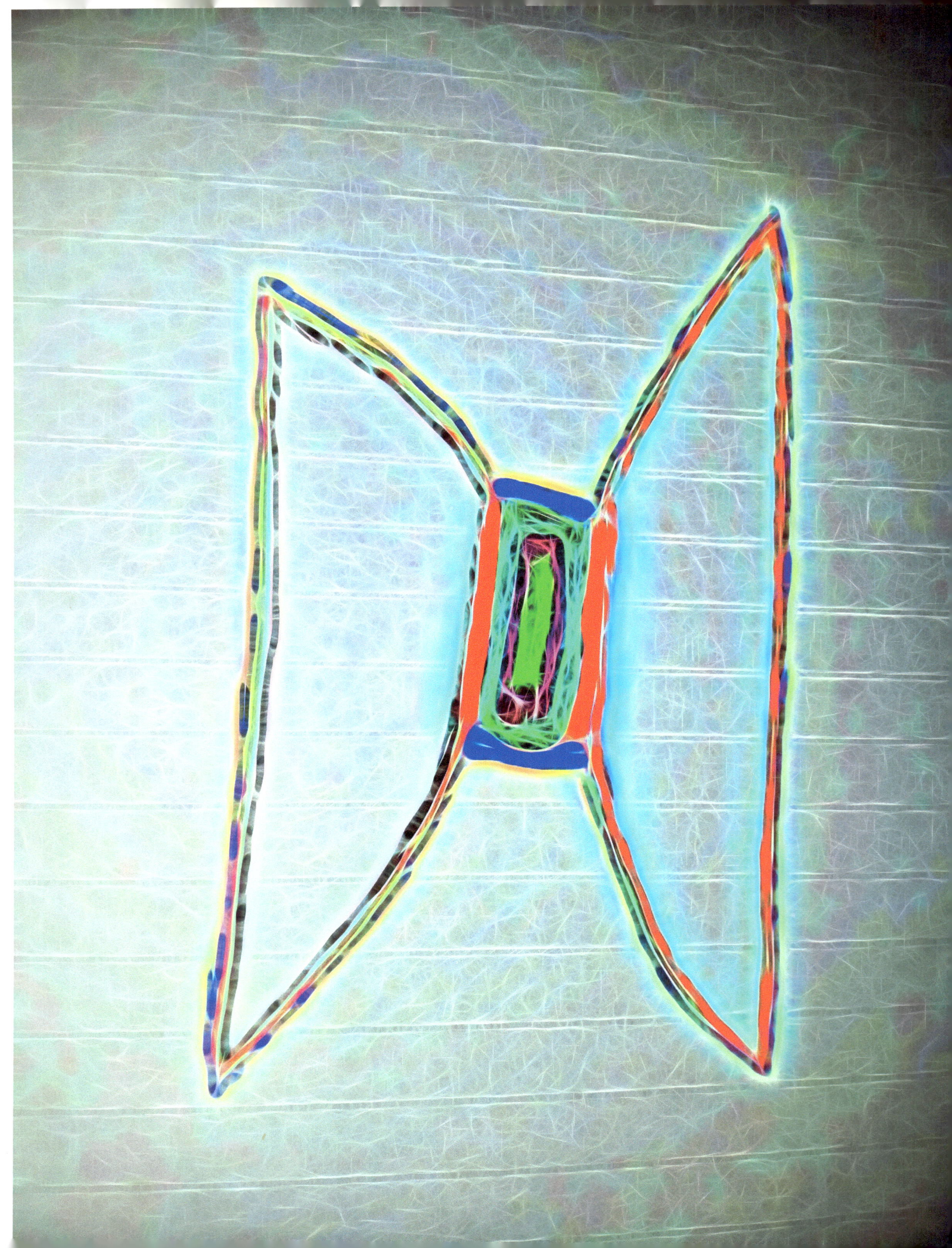

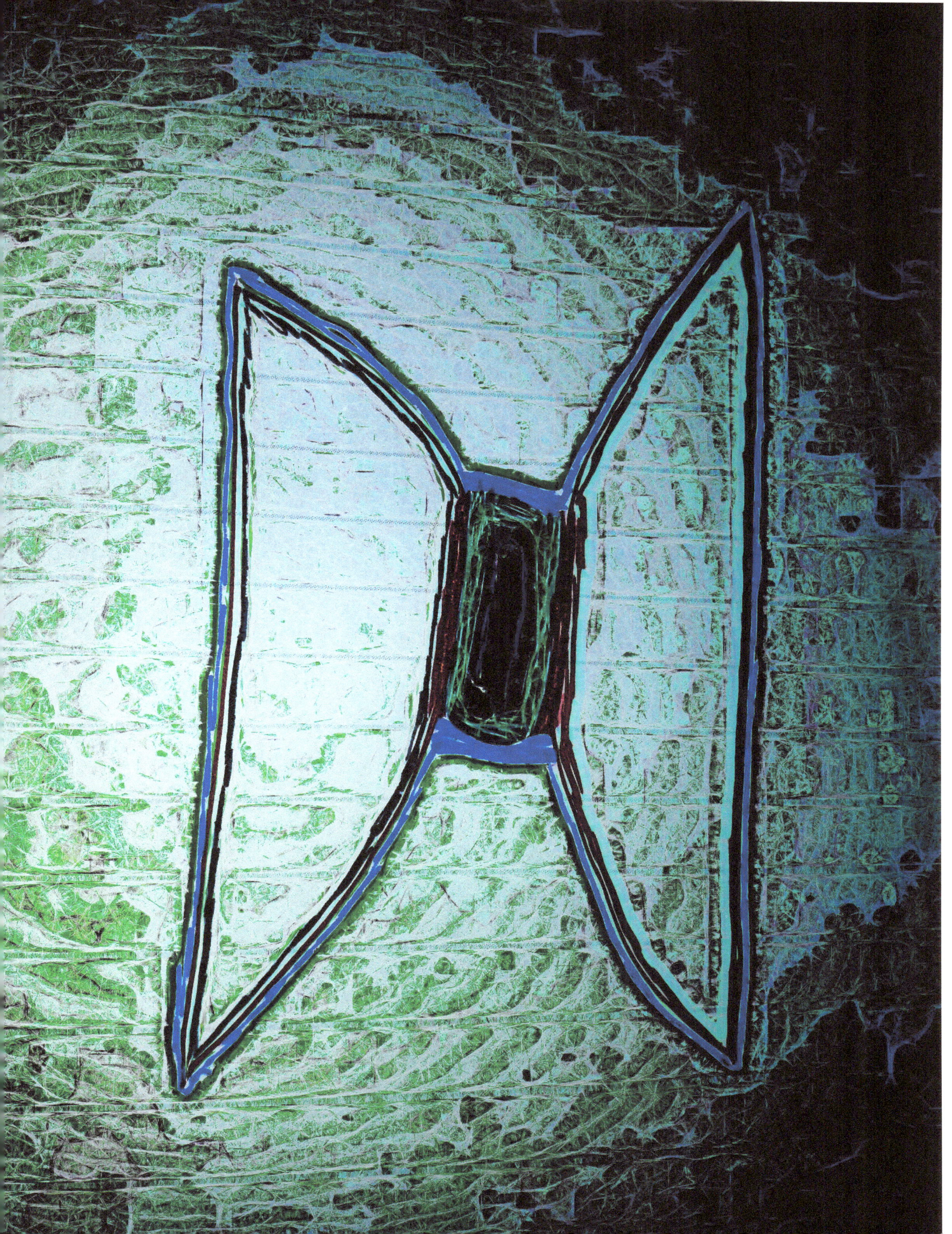

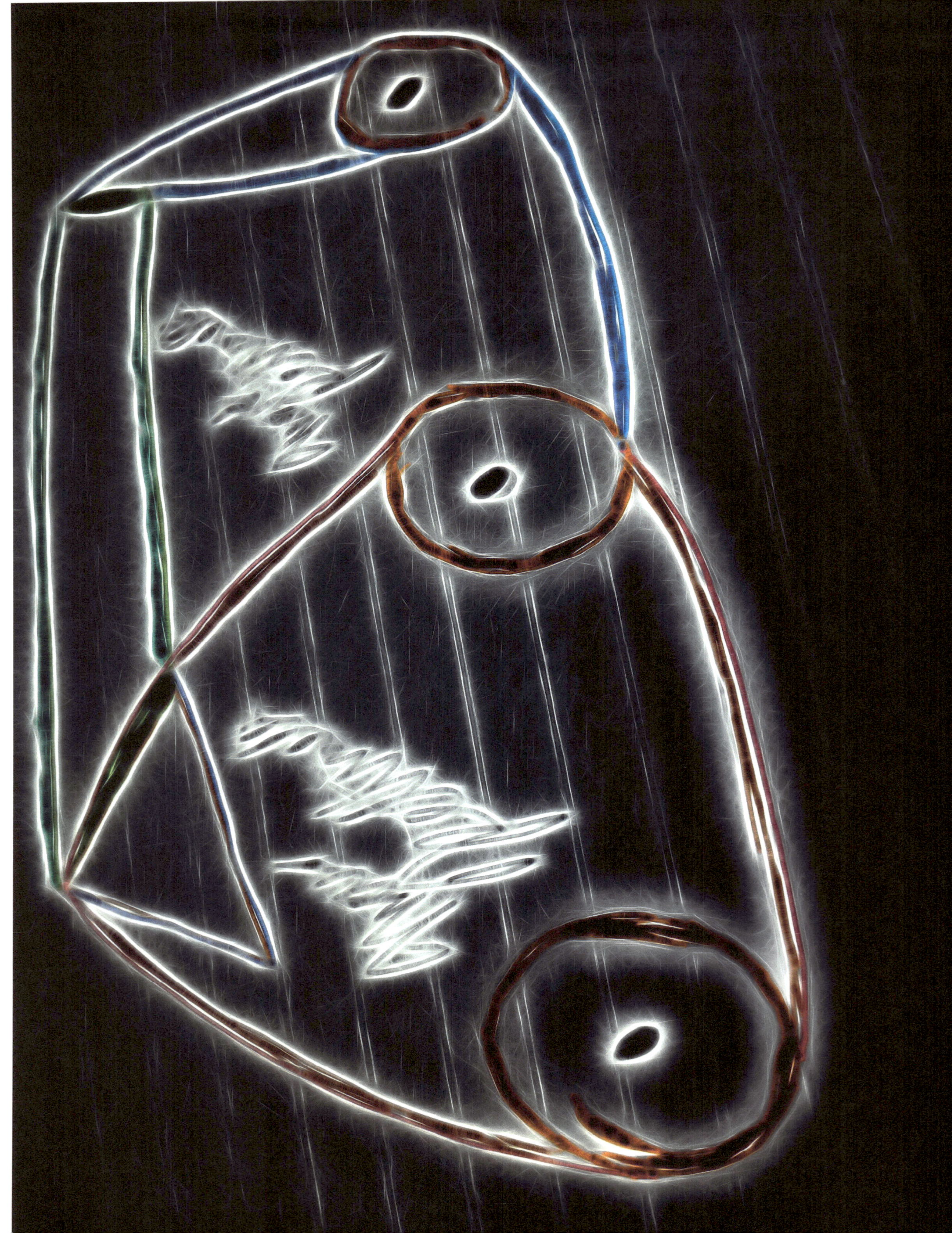

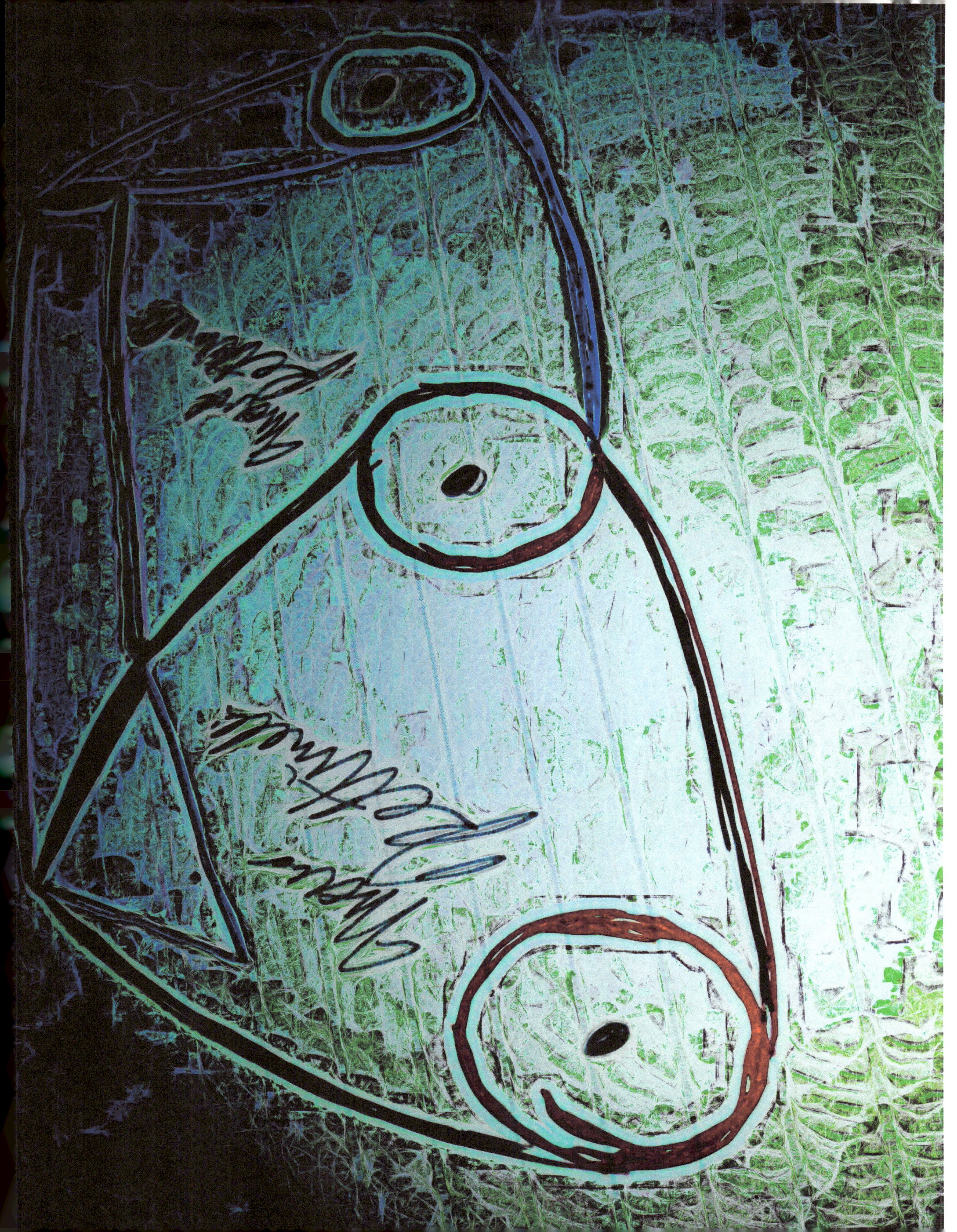

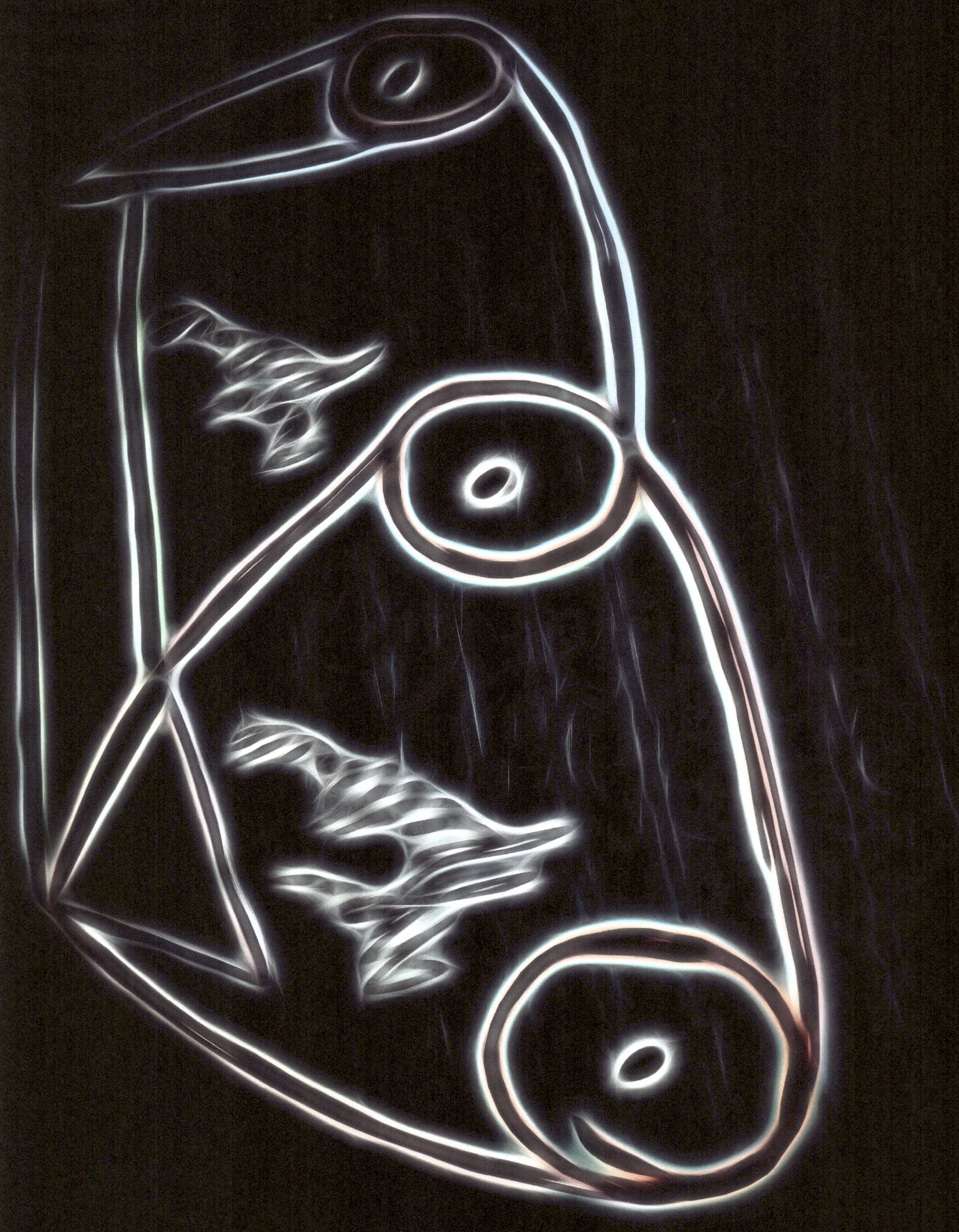

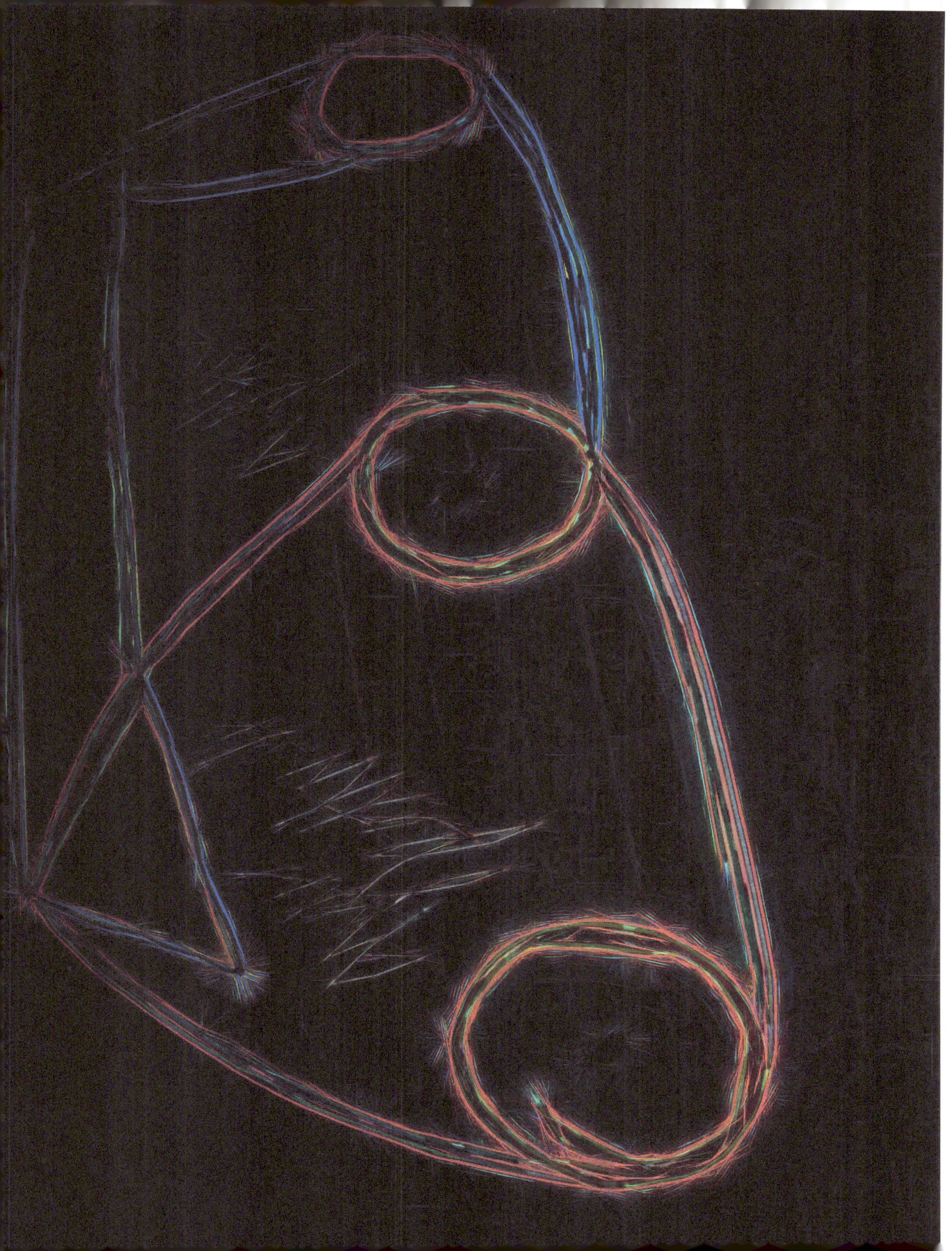

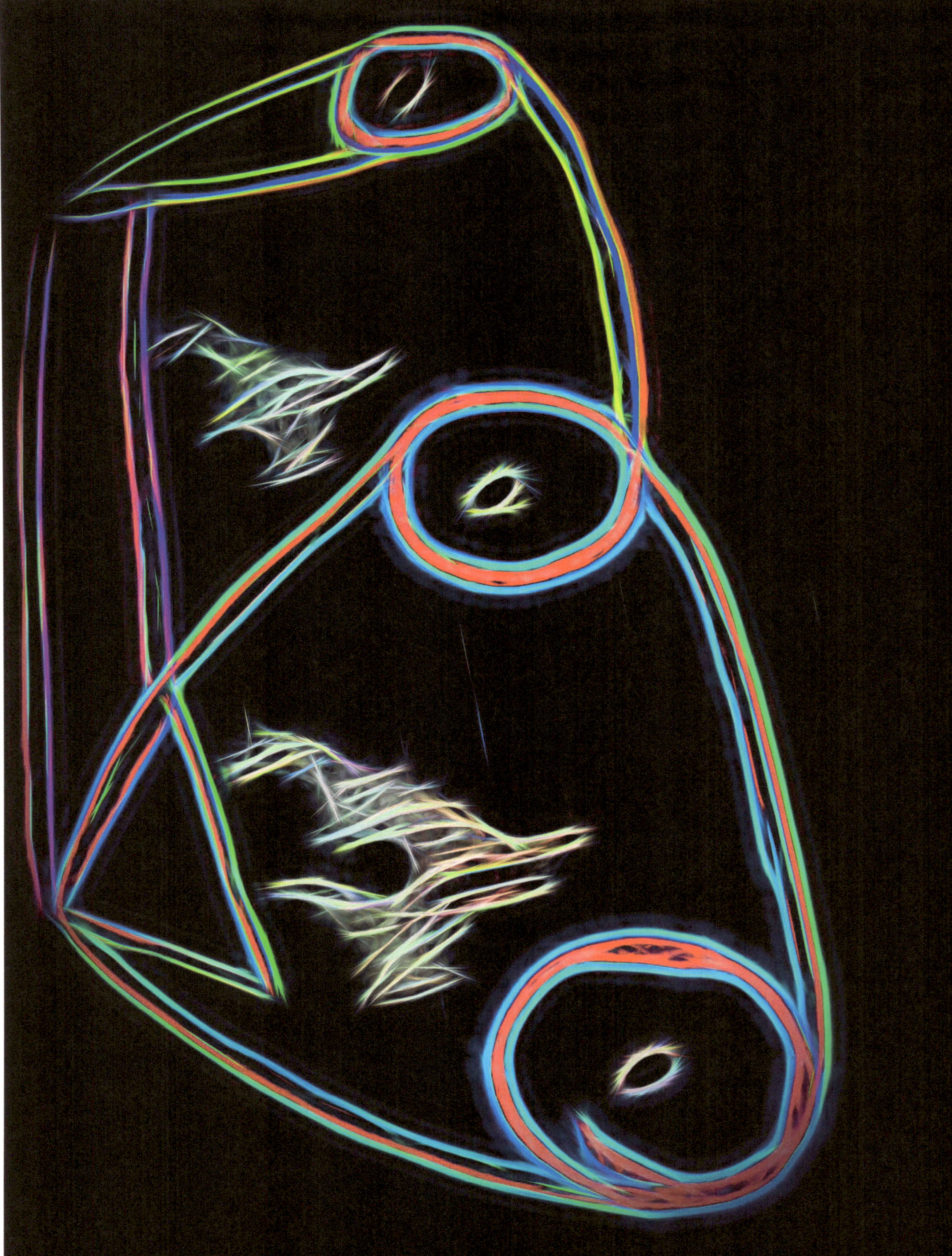

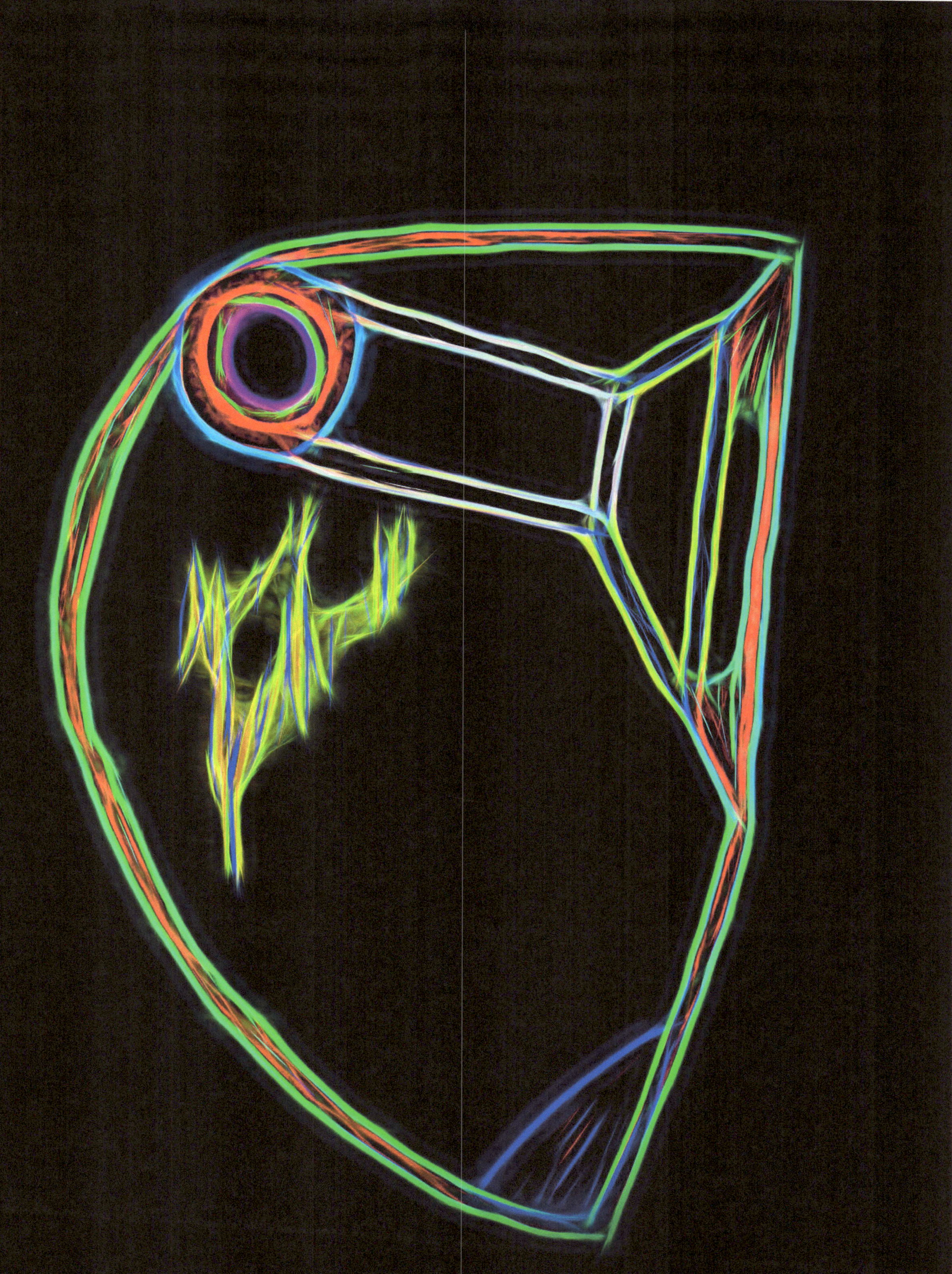

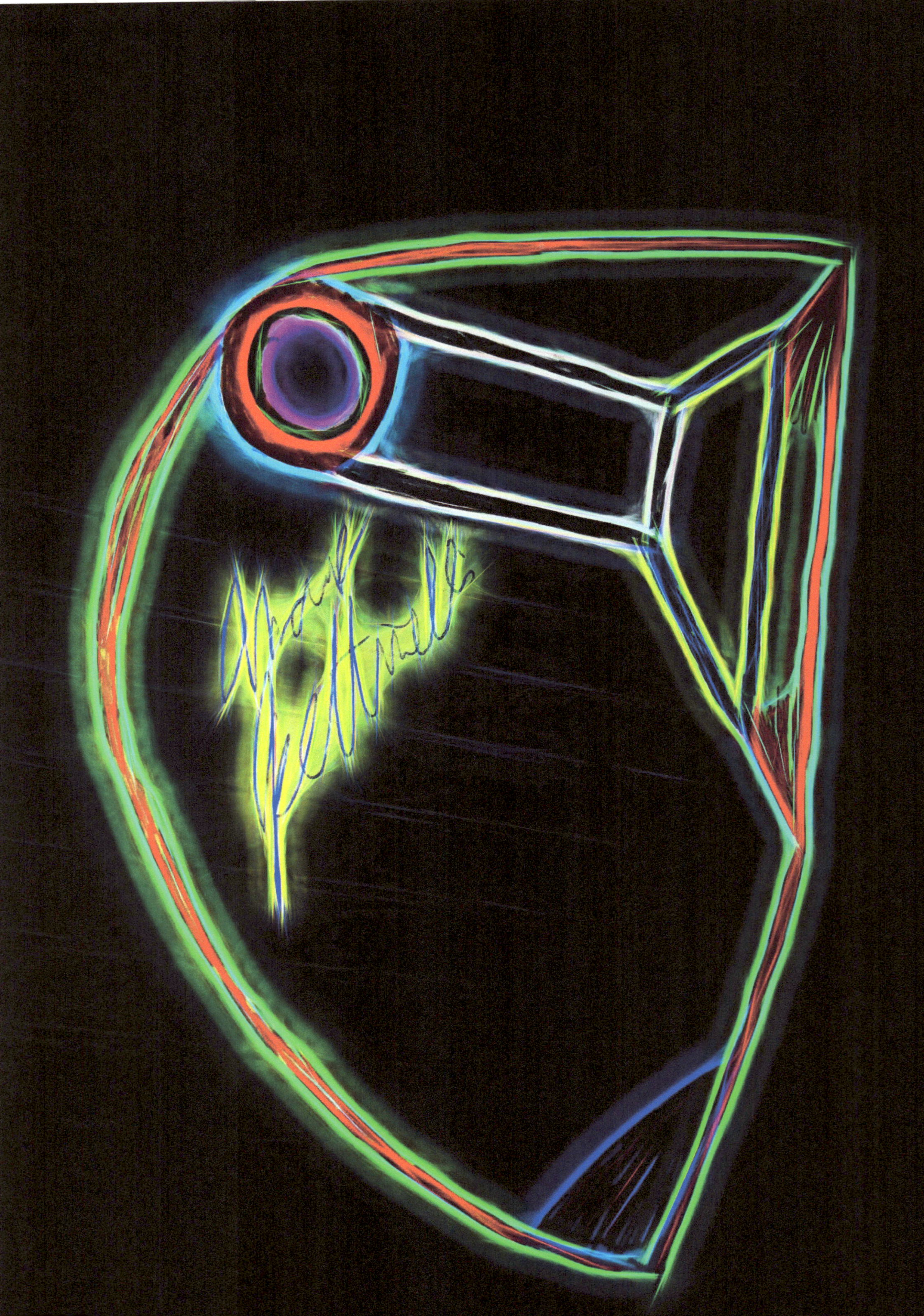

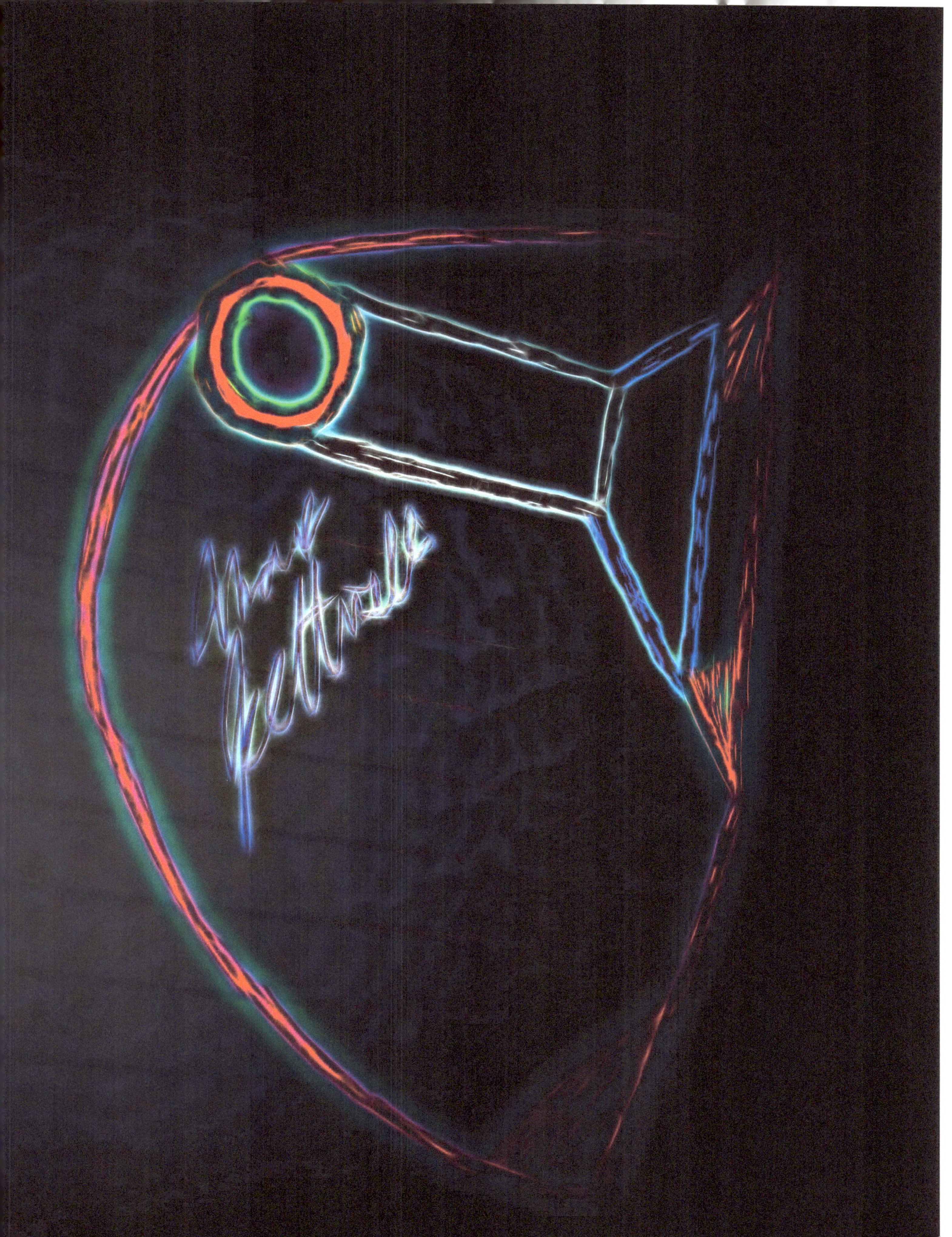

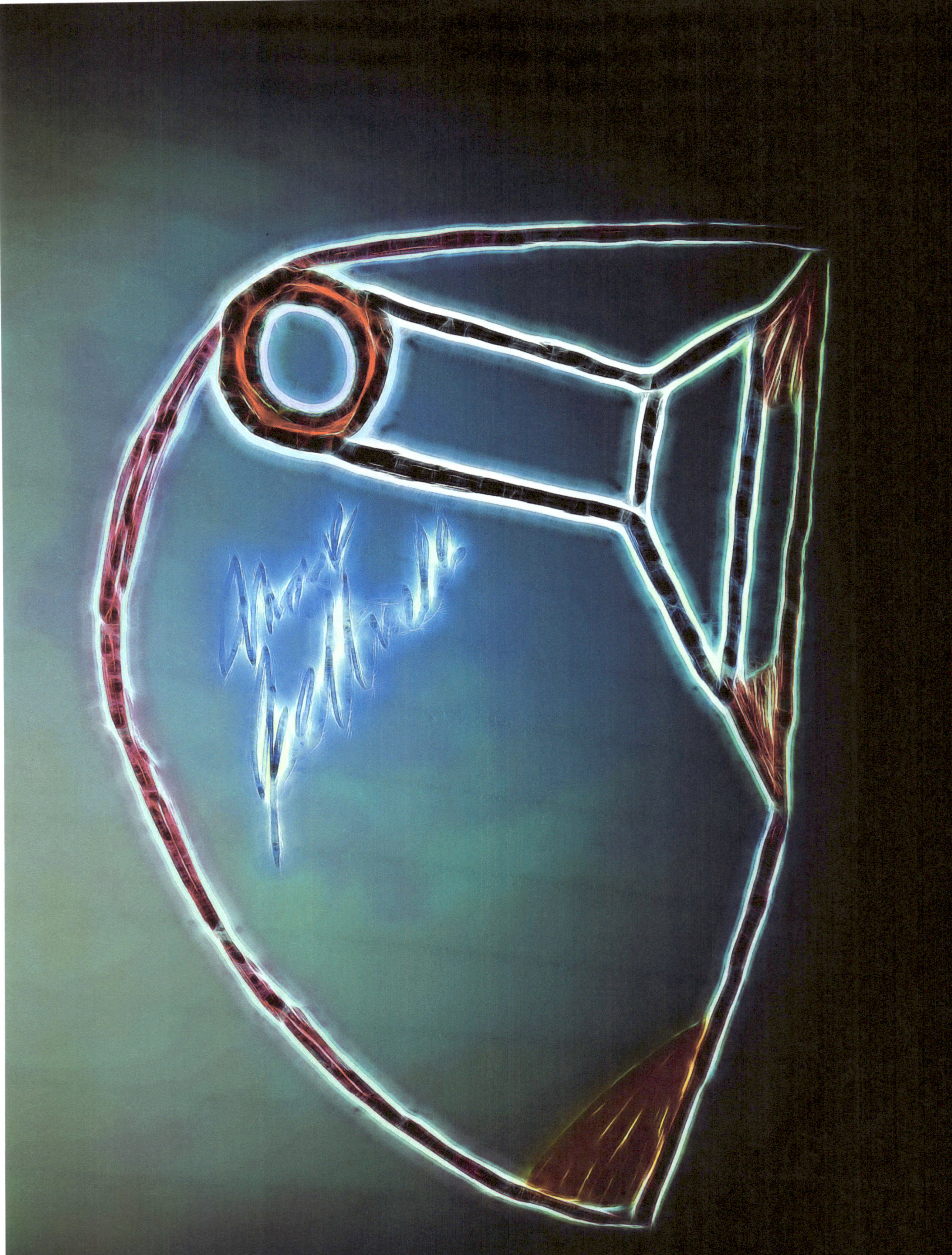

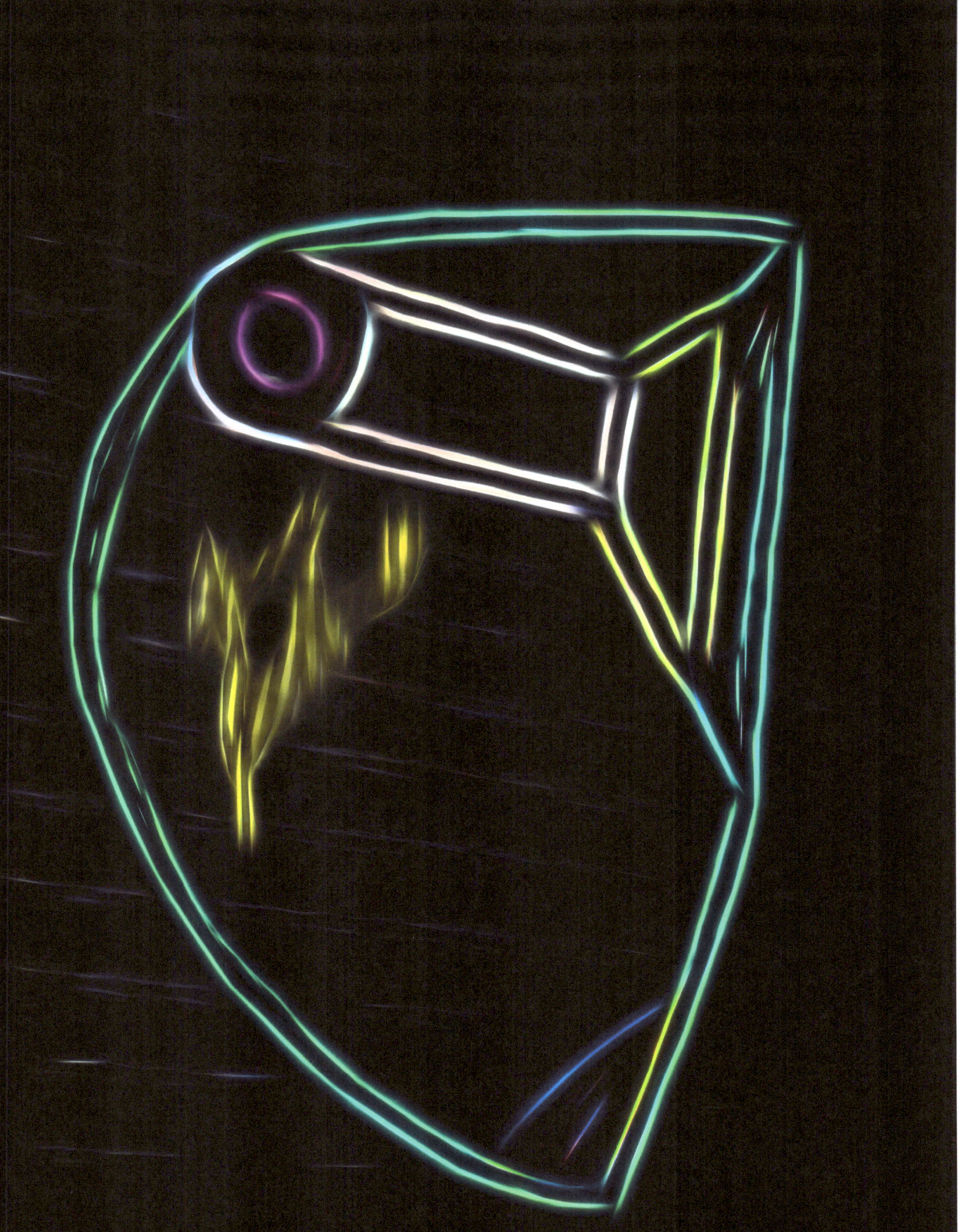

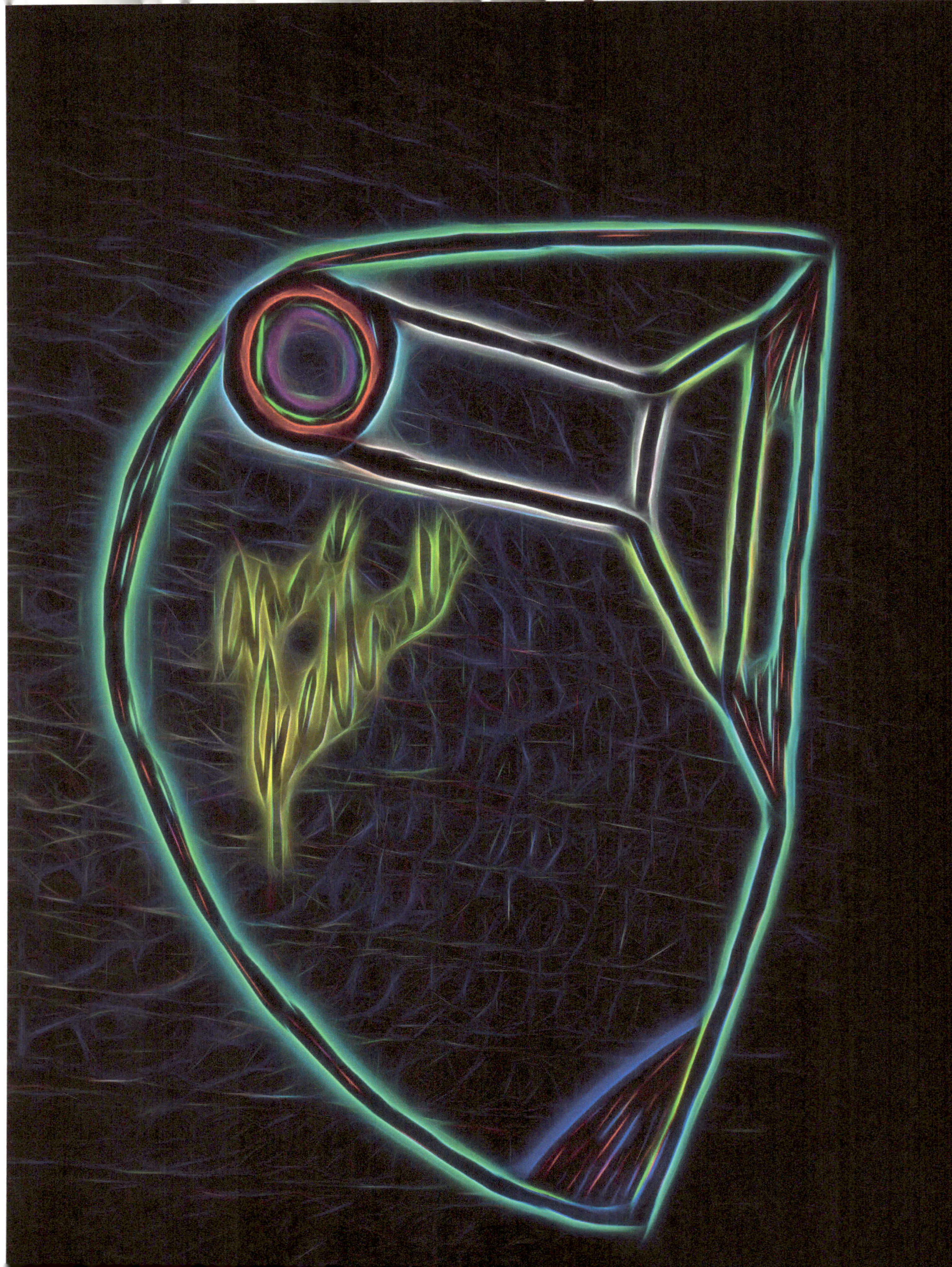

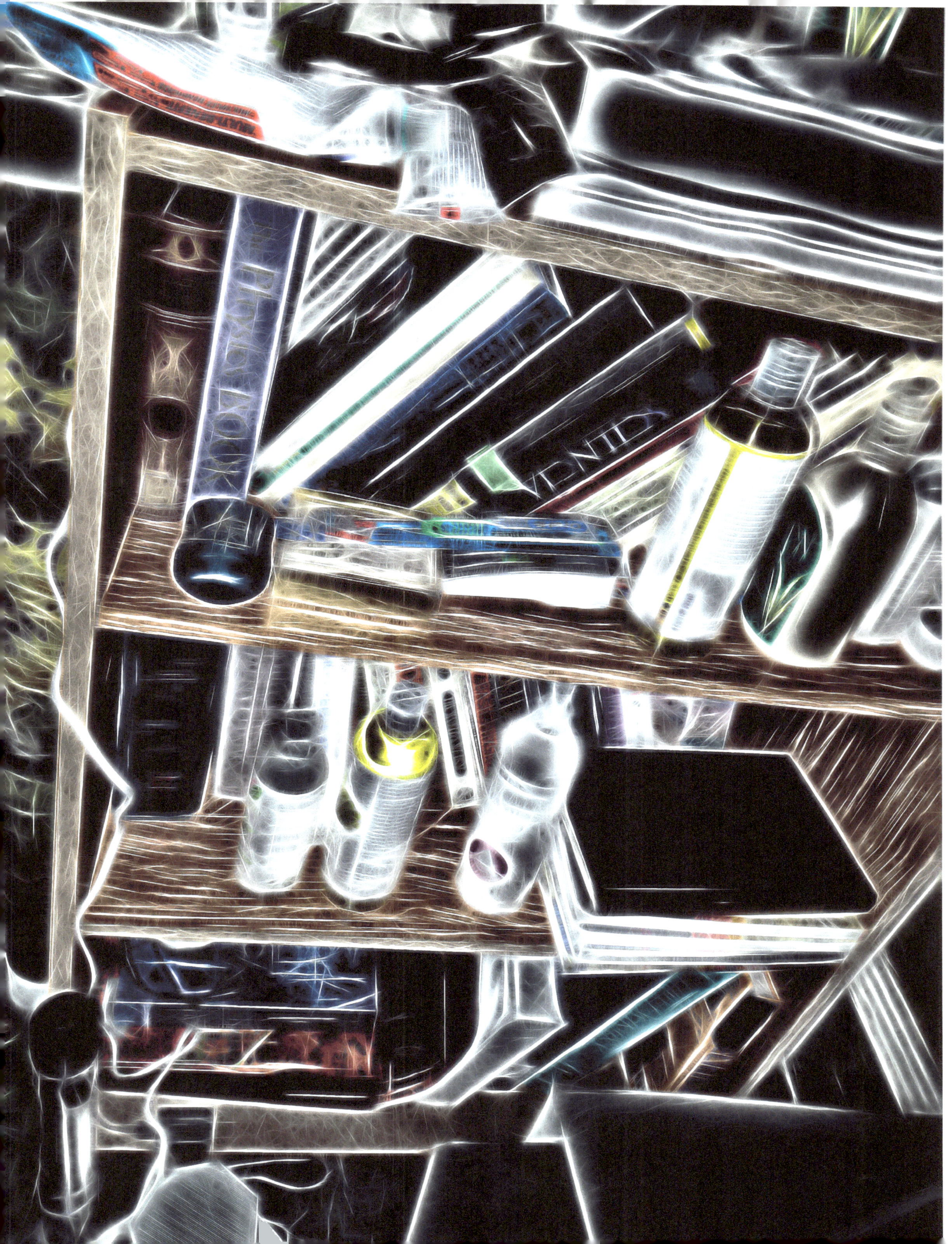

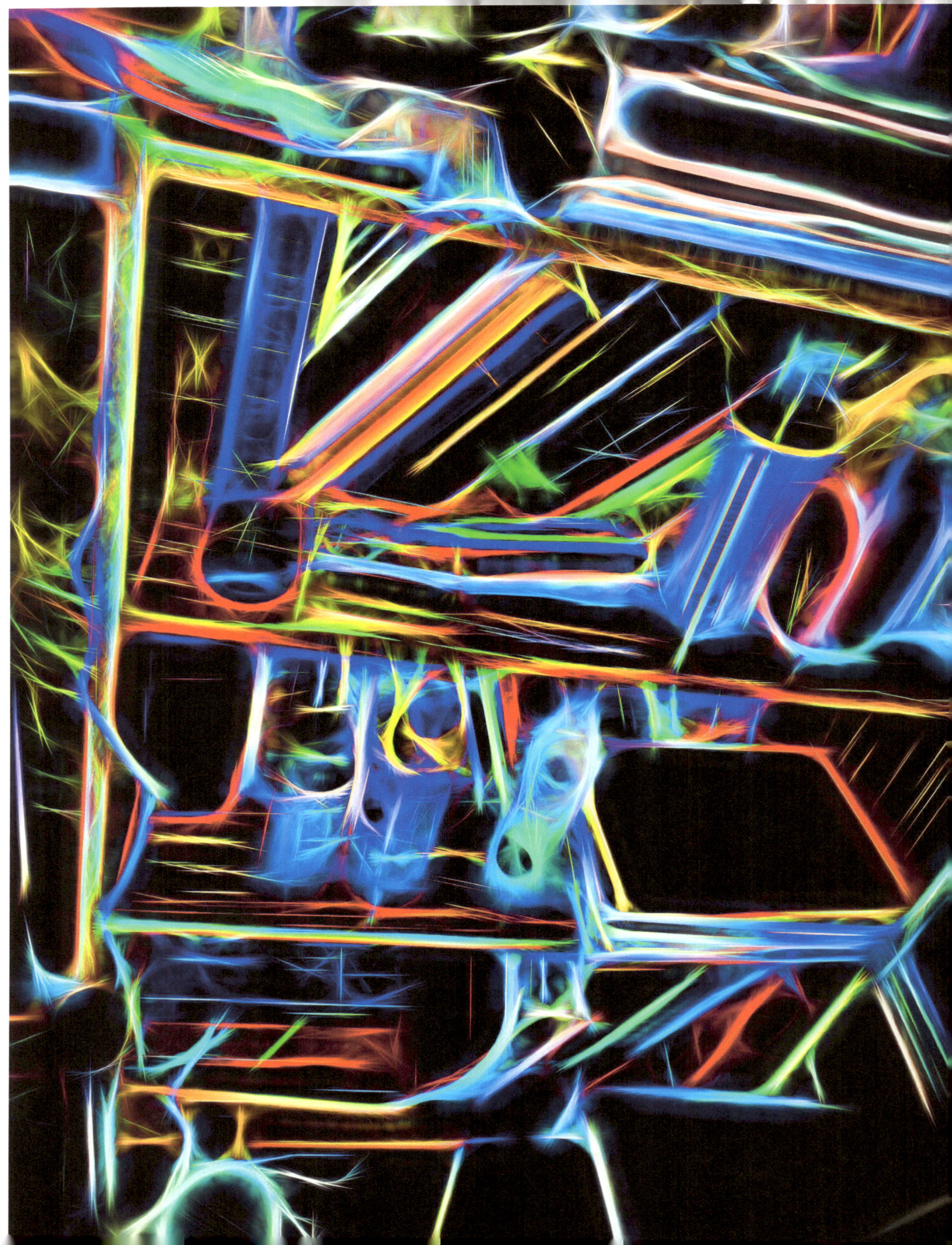

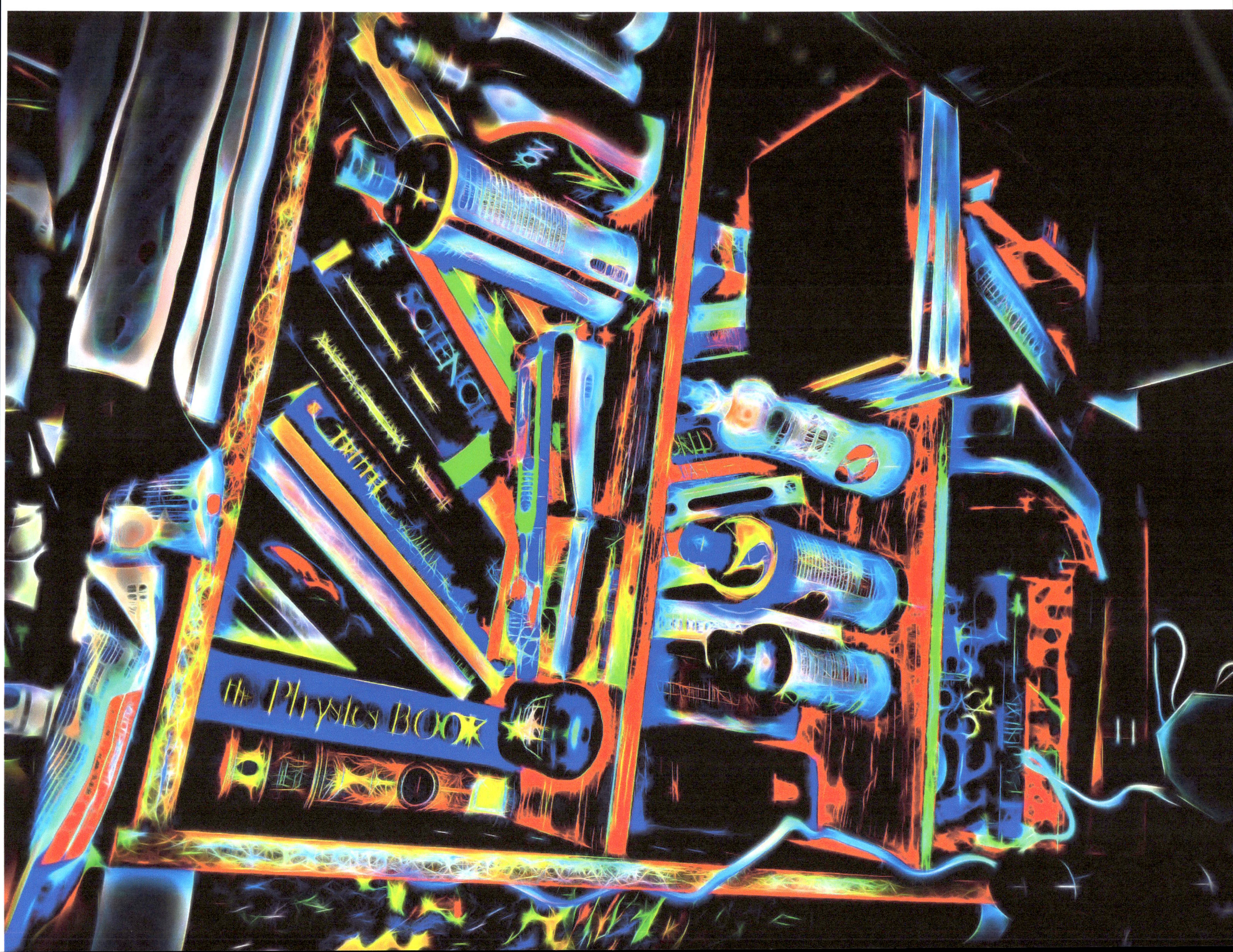

the Physics BOOK
SCIENCE

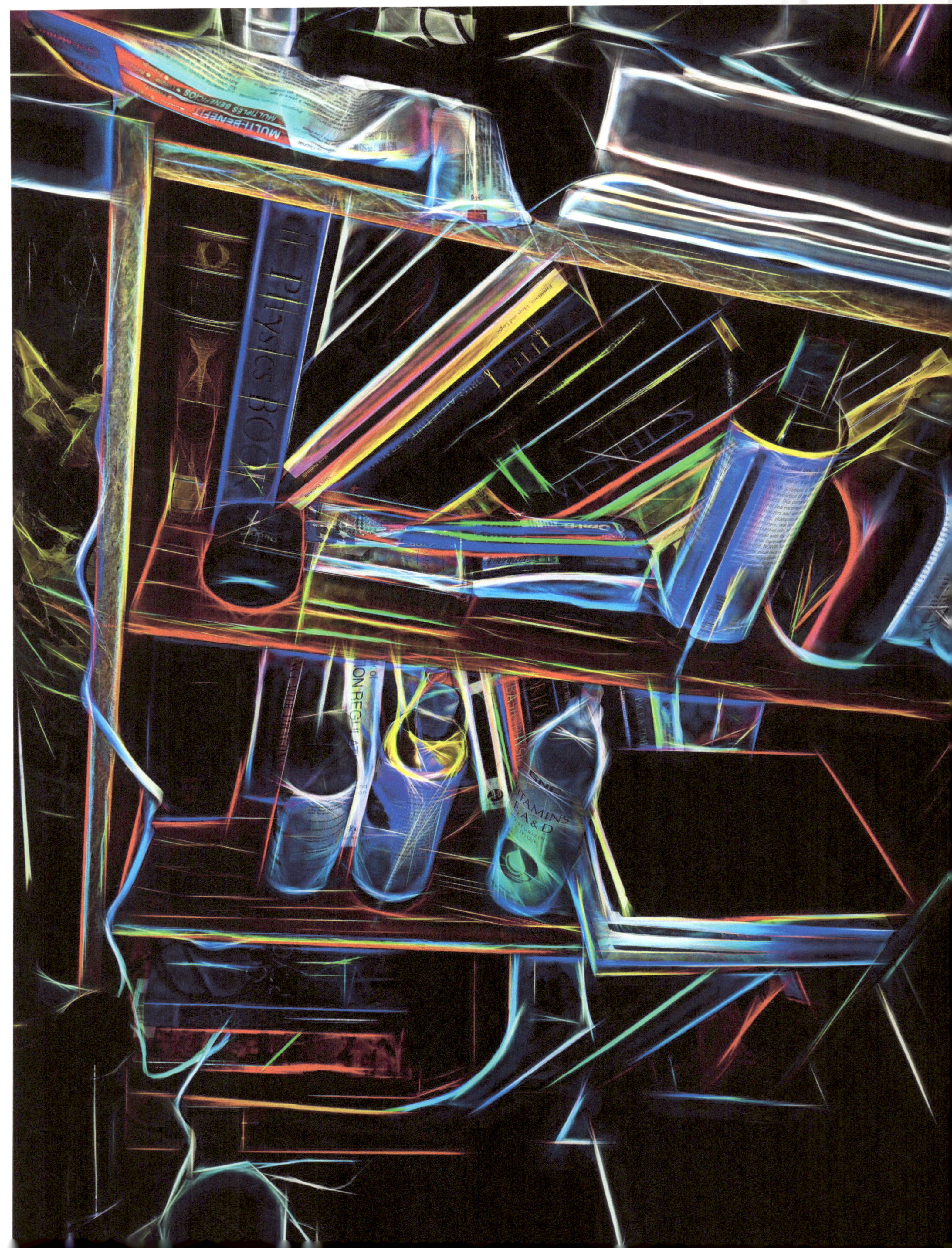

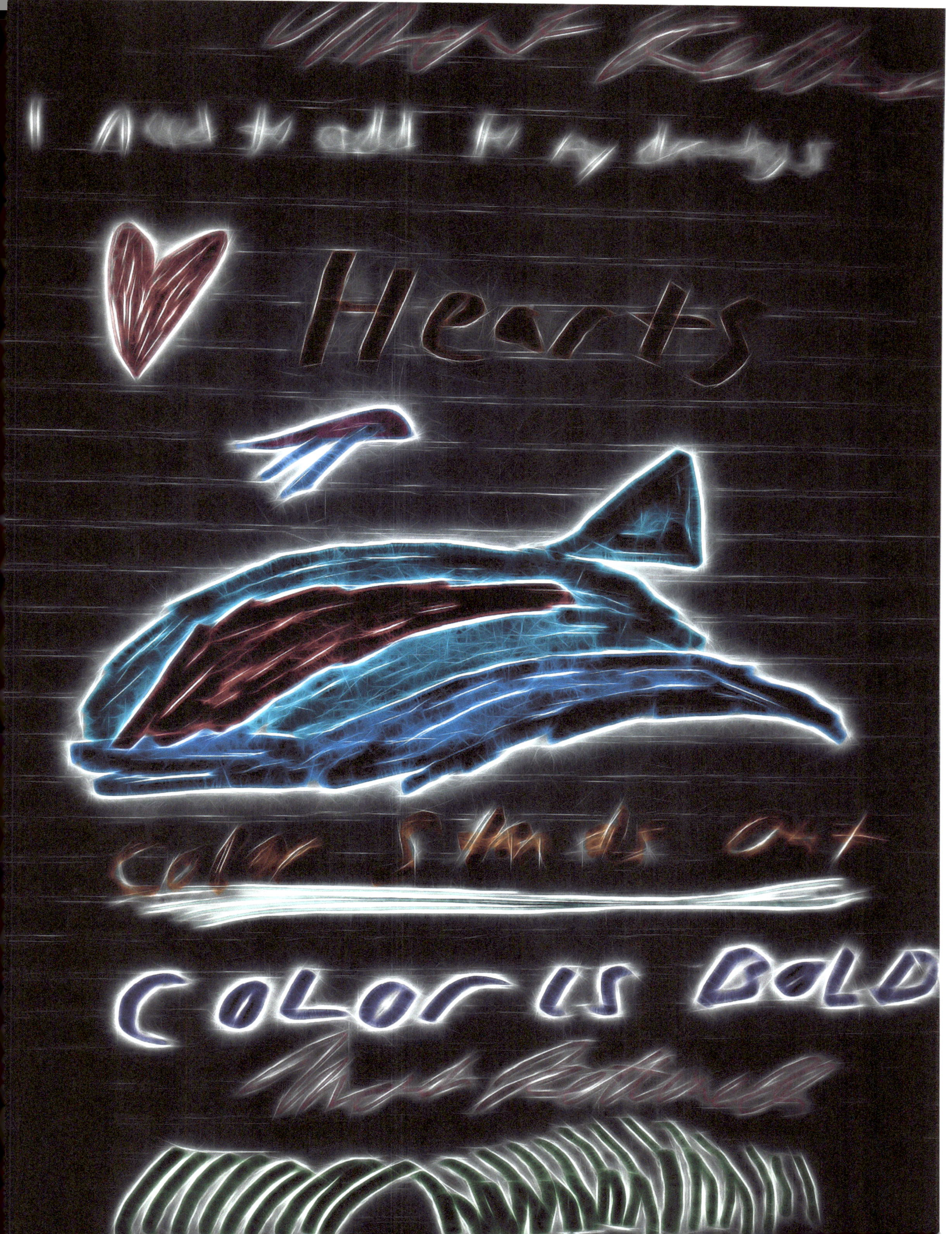
Hearts
Color Stands out
COLOR IS BOLD

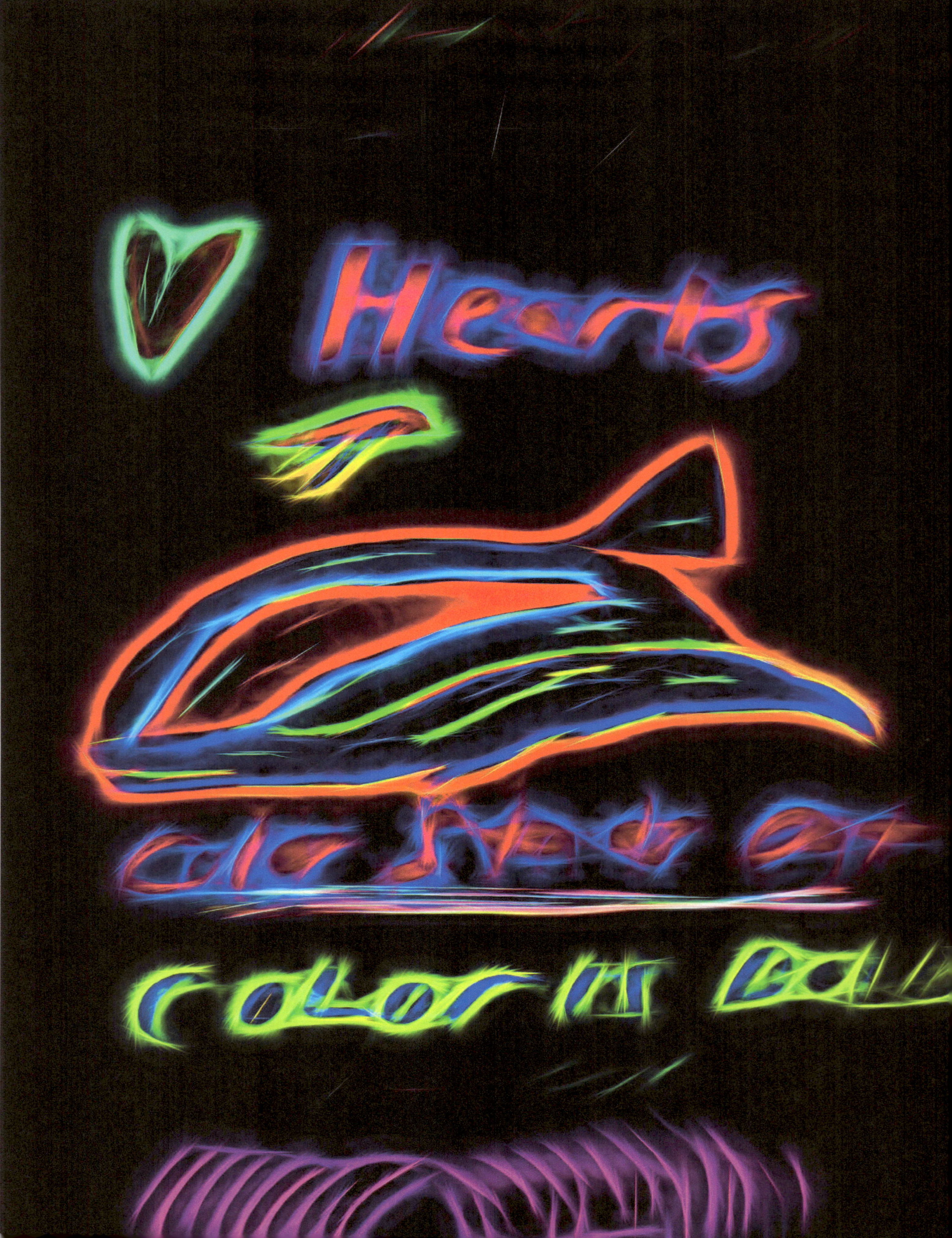

Hearts
COLOR IT DAY

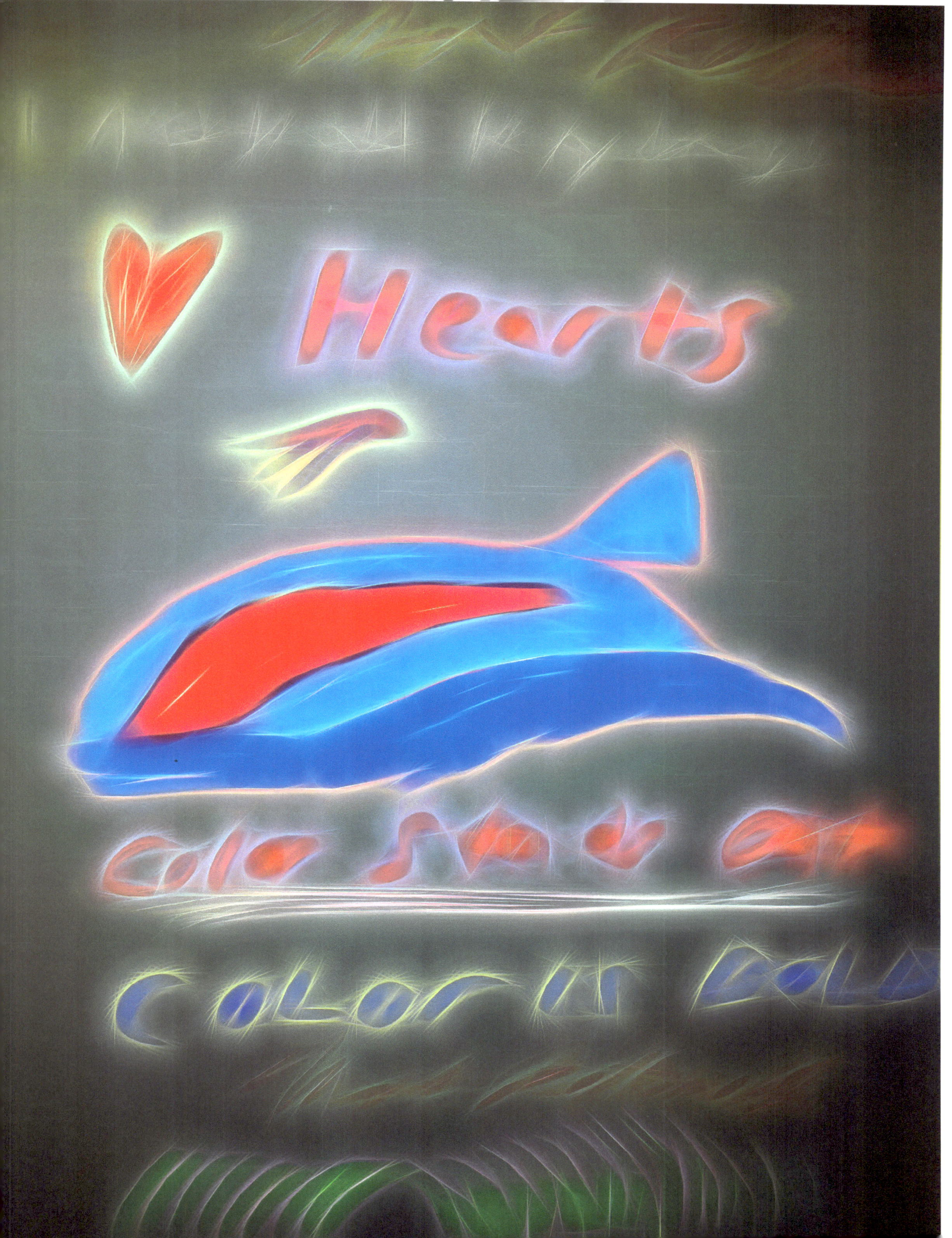
Hearts
Color is bold

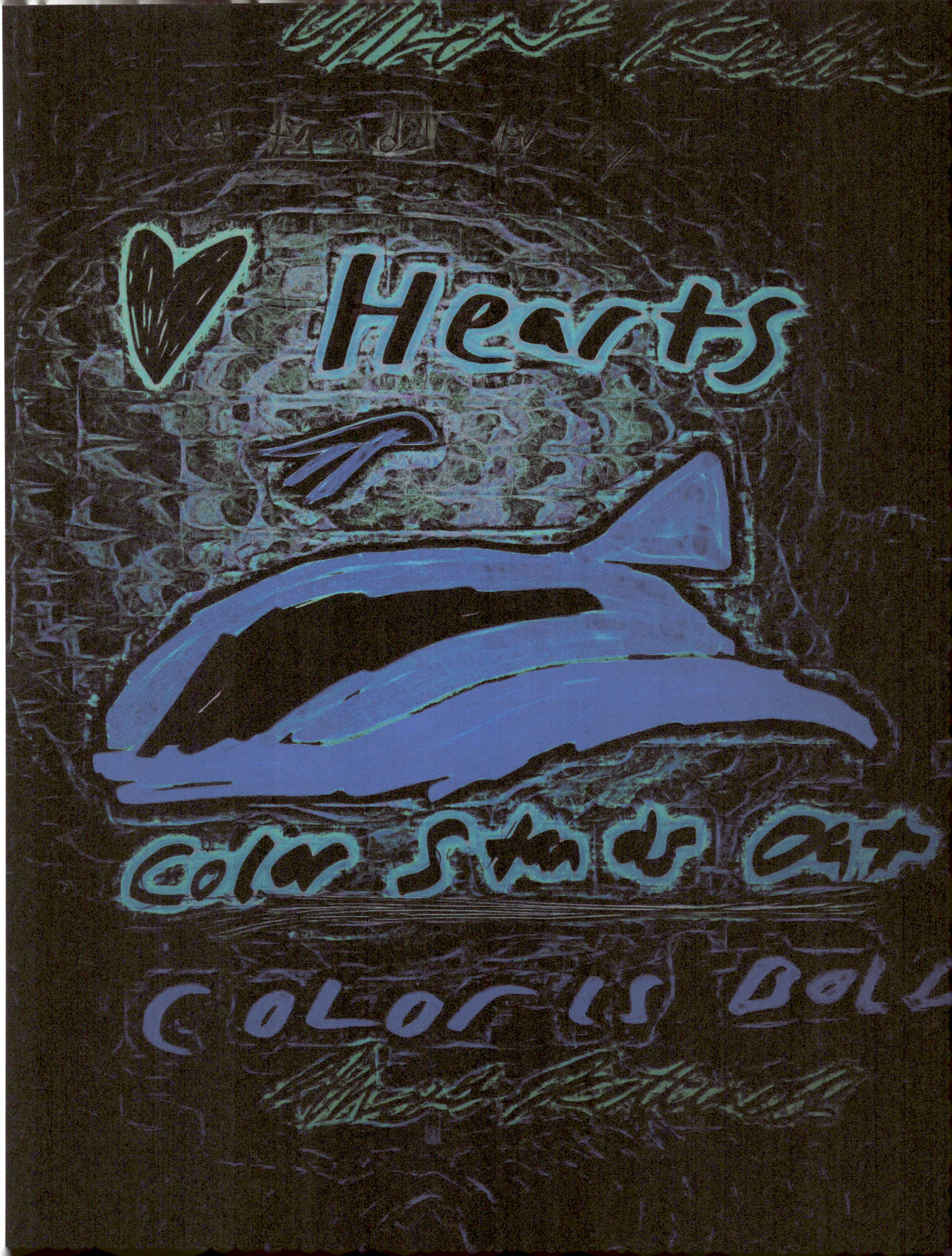

Hearts
color study art
color is bold

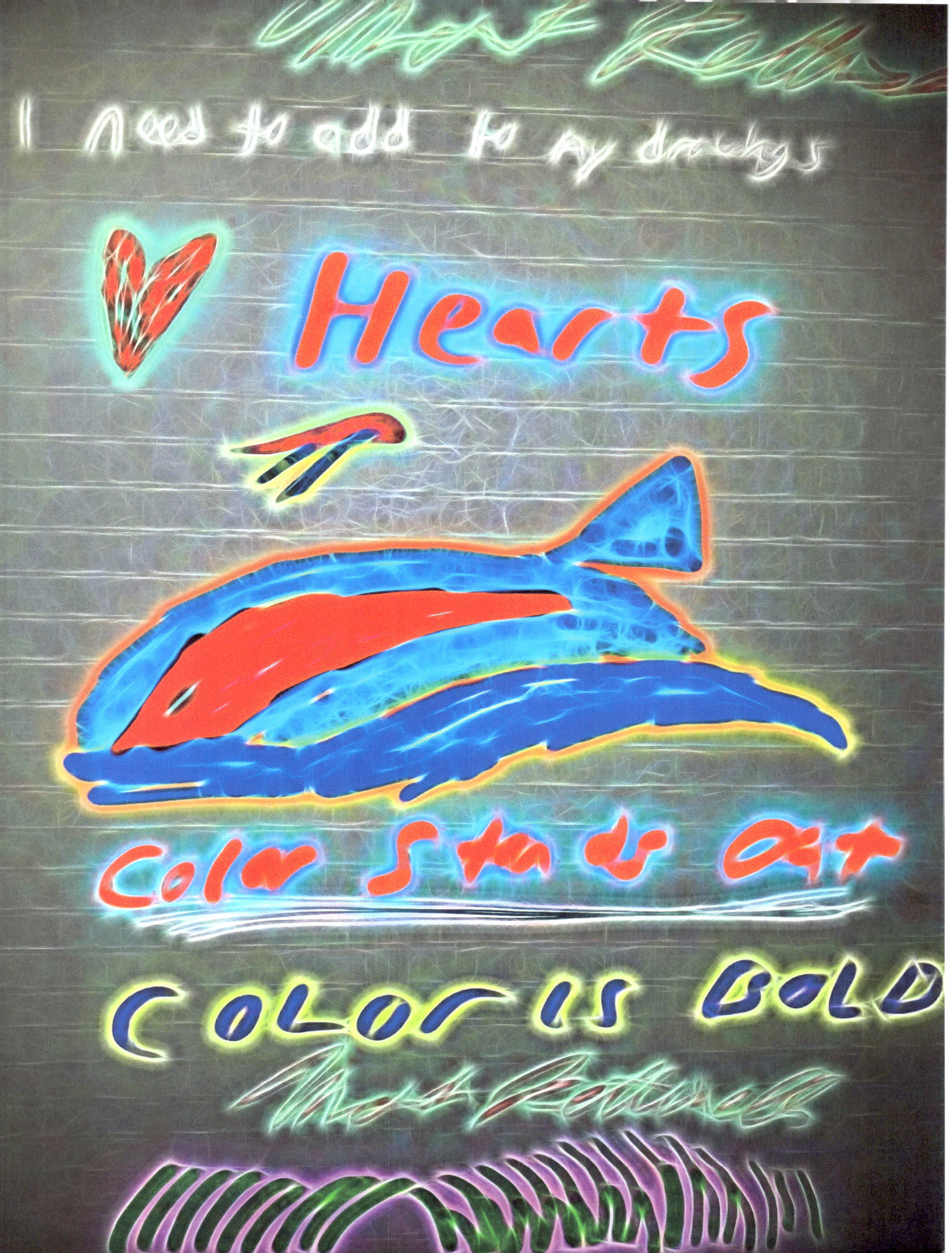

I need to add to my drawings
Hearts
Color Stands Out
COLOR IS BOLD

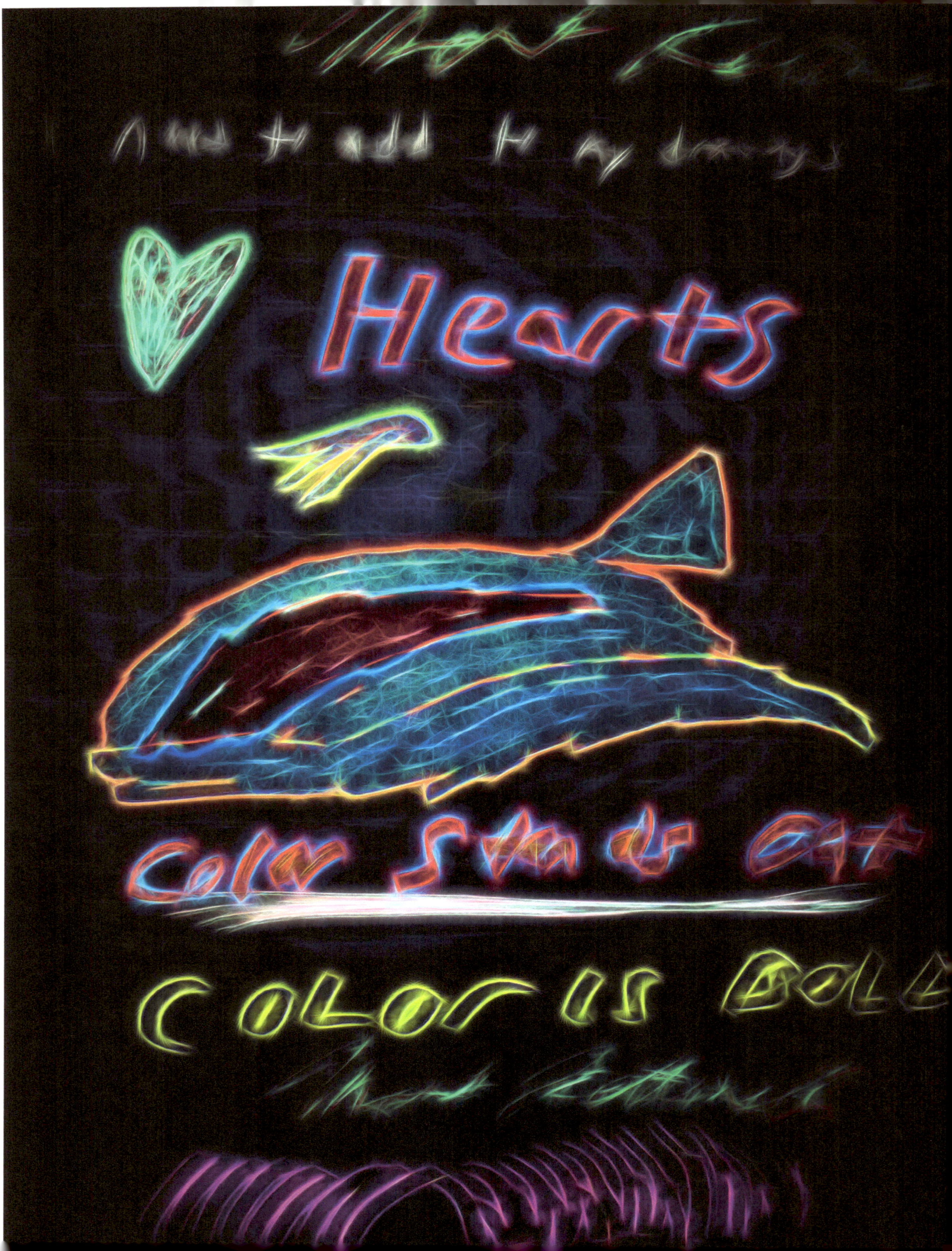

Hearts

COLOR IS BOLD

I need to add to my drawings

Hearts

color stands out

COLOR IS BOLD

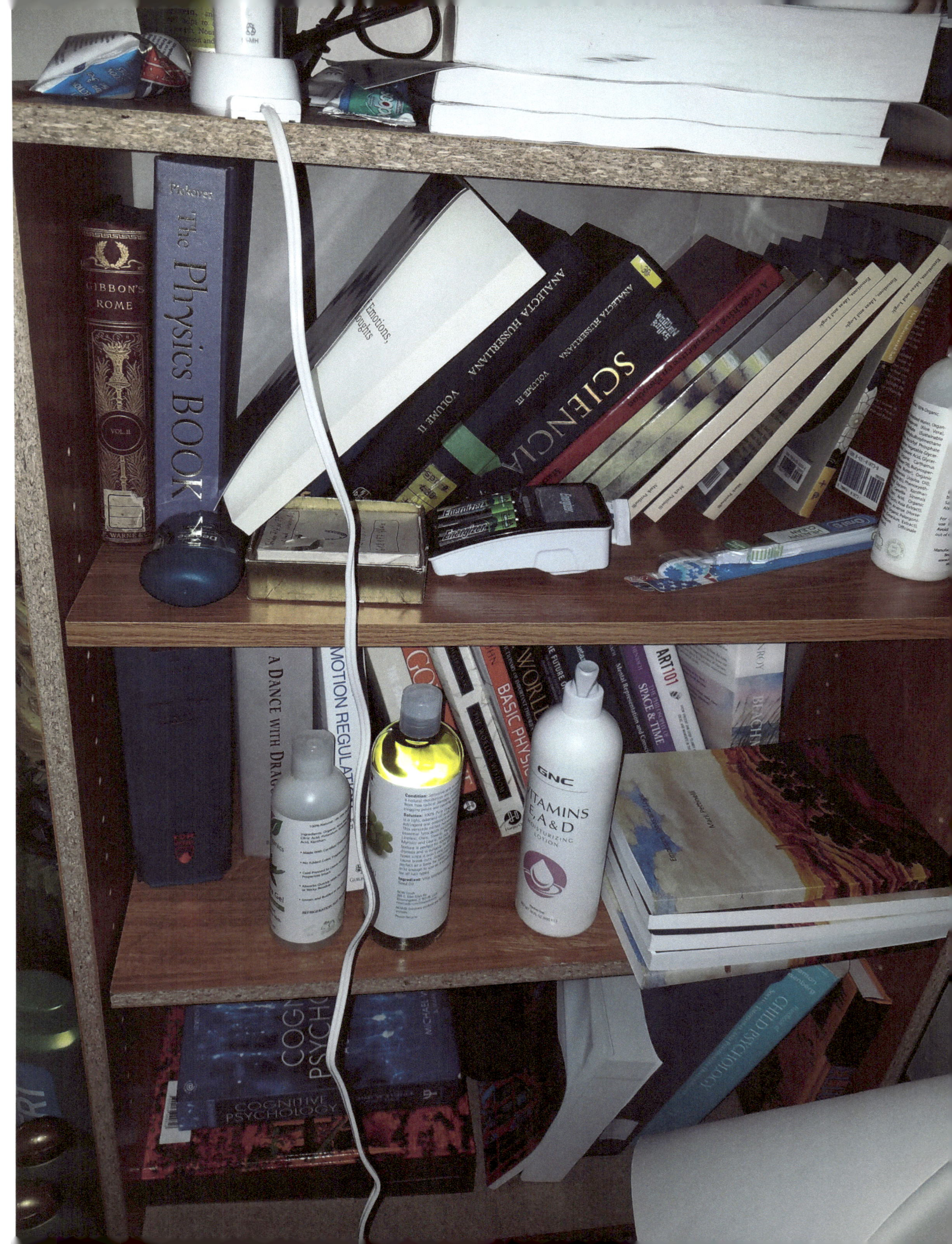

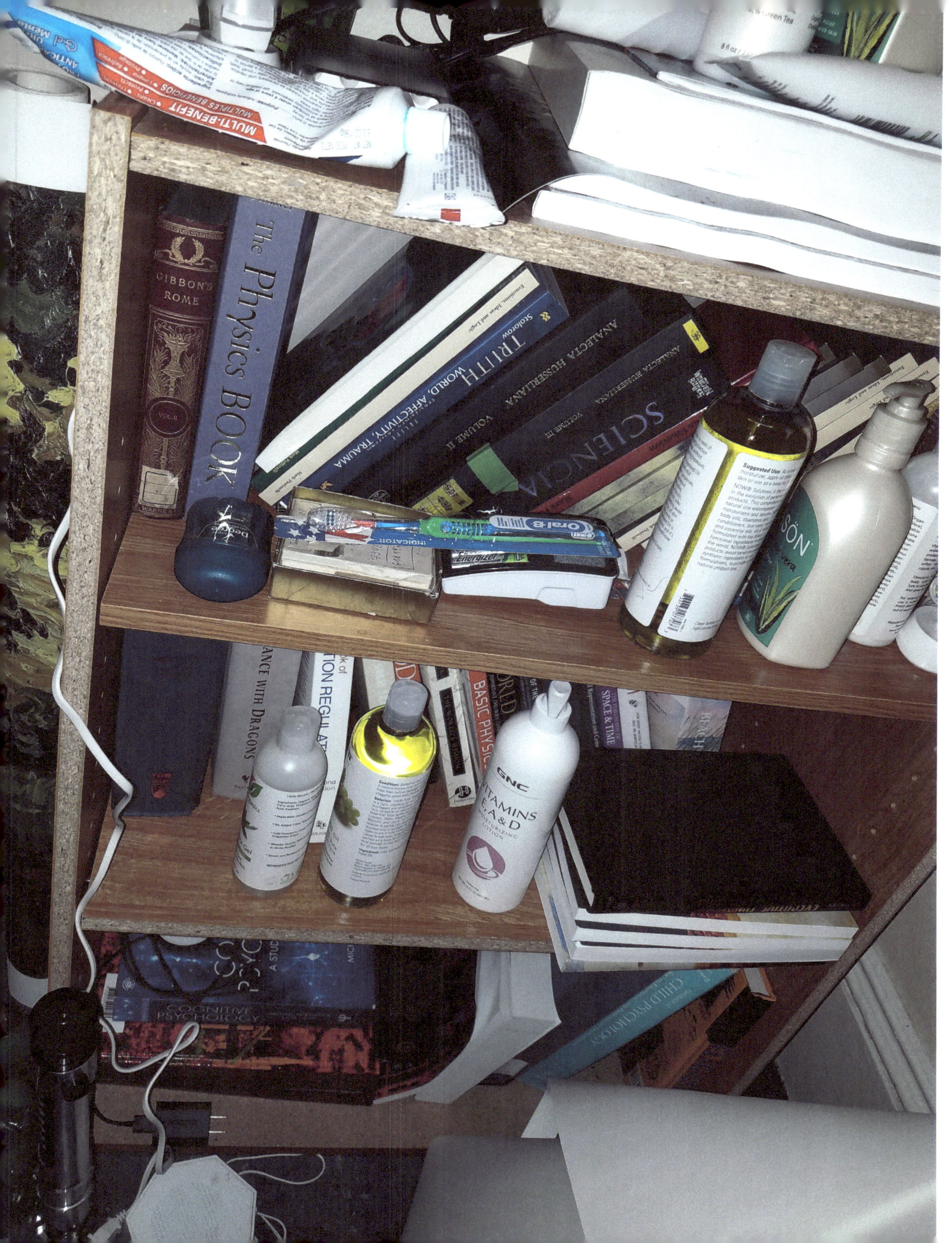

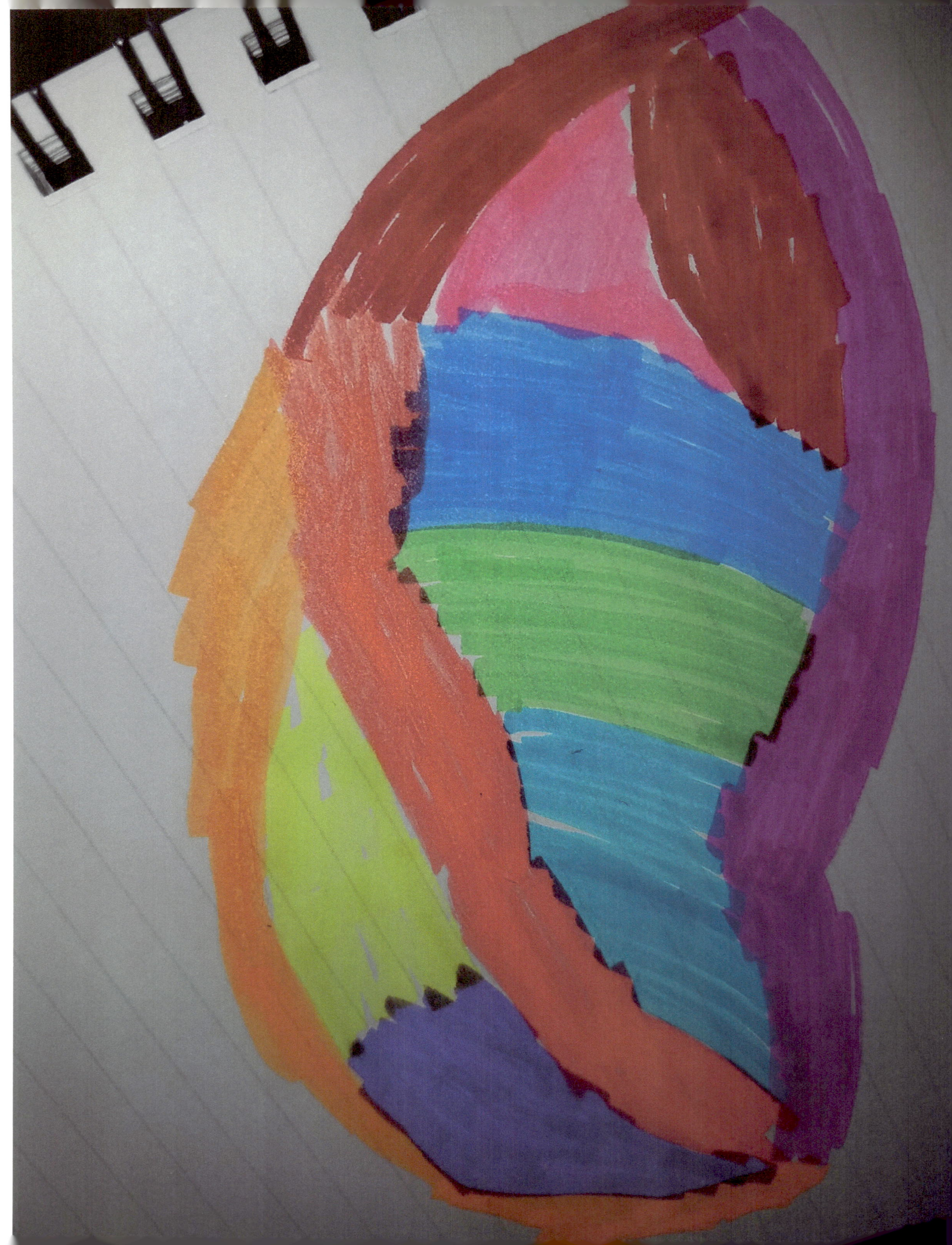